CLAIRE'S ALLOTMENT ESSENTIALS

VOLUME 1 — AN EASY GUIDE TO GROWING YOUR OWN

CLAIRE BURGESS

COPYRIGHT PAGE

First published in Great Britain by Unusually Tall Stories Ltd.

Cover design by Damonza

www.clairesallotment.com
www.unusuallytallstories.com

To Mark, Emily, George, Marilyn Burgess & Walter Miller

CONTENTS

LET'S GET STARTED

BEETROOT

BROAD BEANS

CARROTS

CONTAINER GARDENING AND RAISED BEDS

COURGETTES

FRENCH BEANS

ONIONS

POTATOES

PARSNIPS

RADISHES

STRAWBERRIES

TOMATOES

LET'S GET STARTED

INTRODUCTION

Growing fruit and vegetables, I think, is one of the most rewarding things you can do.

Whether you're growing just for yourself, your family, friends or on a huge scale as a business.

When you sow your seeds and they emerge through the soil at the beginning of the season, then you nurture them as they grow, and finally, they produce something that you can pick and eat is just marvellous.

I sowed my very first seeds when I was about seven years old, which were some radish, and I've been hooked ever since.

In all the places that I've lived, with either my parents or with my husband and now our two children, I have always managed to grow something. Sometimes it's just been tomatoes in pots in the sun lounge, or courgettes outside in a large pot. Sometimes it's been strawberries in my little patch of soil in my parents' garden when I was very young and still lived at home, or on my allotment that I had for twelve years, and now in raised beds in the back garden of our new home.

You can grow fruit and vegetables anywhere, even if you don't have access to any space outside. Use a sunny window sill, where you can grow some salad leaves, or some herbs, or maybe even a bush tomato plant. My books will help you on your growing journey and make growing fruit and vegetables easy. You don't have to sow your plants from seed, just pop to your local garden centre and buy a small plant or two and then nurture them once you get back home.

The taste of freshly harvested produce can't even be described, but I'll try. The flavour explosion that happens in your mouth is amazing. It's then that you realise what they're supposed to taste like.

WHAT DO YOU WANT TO GROW?

Before you even start digging you must think about the following:

What do I want to grow?

Don't have your plans set in stone, just have a rough plan. After all a plan is just a guideline, and things can and will always change.

If it's your first time growing, then I suggest that you write down a short list of a combination of about five or six fruits and vegetables that you would really like to grow.

Personally I would suggest easy ones like: potatoes, onions, carrots, tomatoes, french beans, courgettes, radish, strawberries or beetroot.

Obviously, if there is something else you eat on a regular basis, then put that down, but don't try anything too complicated in your first year. If you feel that three or four items will be enough for you, then that's absolutely fine.

Don't feel that you have to buy seeds for all these, you can usually buy small plants of most of the ones I've suggested. Just follow the instructions that come with them to see what you need to do.

HOW MUCH SPACE DO I NEED?

It's always best to start small, then you can always increase the area you garden. With regards to an allotment, there's nothing worse that having loads of space, and then having over half of it becoming overgrown. This can get very depressing and then you'll feel like you're unable to cope and get disheartened.

Always have a small patch, and wish you have more space.

Gardening is supposed to be enjoyable and not a chore, so think about how much time you have to "play" in your garden.

You don't want to spend all your free time weeding and tidying your gardening area. You need to make sure you also have plenty of time in which you can enjoy it as well, and sit down on a lazy summer's day and gaze at the magnificence of it.

BASIC TOOLS YOU'LL NEED TO GET STARTED.

There are some basic tools that you'll need before you even break the soil. Just get a few to start with and then you can gradually increase your collection.

If you've got a birthday or Christmas coming up, then new tools are ideal gifts for people to buy you. But make sure you specify which exact ones you'd like. Or, alternatively ask for garden centre vouchers and then you can go and get exactly what you need.

As a general rule don't go for the cheap tools as they'll break within five minutes of you using them. Well, they do for me. Maybe I'm just too rough with them.

Here is what you need and a few little tips before you buy:

Large garden fork - Make sure the bottom half of the handle is stainless steel and the top half is wooden. If the entire handle is wooden it will break because of the force at the top of the prongs when you dig. Make sure there are four prongs on the fork and they are fairly long. The best one I would suggest is a **Gardman Digging Fork**, which you should be able to find for about £30.

Large garden spade - The same principle as the large fork with regards to the handle, as the force you use when digging will break a weak handle very quickly. Again I would suggest the **Gardman Digging Spade**, which also costs about £30. Don't be tempted to get a **shovel** instead, as they are no good for digging as the blade is curved and nowhere near as sharp as a spade. A shovel won't be able to cut into the soil.

Small hand fork - Please, oh please, don't go for the cheap option when buying one of these. I made that mistake once, it cost me £4.99. I put it in the soil, pulled it back and the handle bent and broke! I never made that mistake again. So, make sure you buy a decent hand fork otherwise you'll end up spending more money in the long run.

You must buy a decent hand fork, there is no getting away from it.

You need to have a comfortable handle, preferably wooden and the fork must have three prongs. You can get ones with four prongs, but those prongs are usually very thin and I prefer fat prongs. I've got a **Burgon & Ball hand fork** and have had it for years. It's very sturdy and does what I need it to do. They cost about £10.

. . .

Hand Trowel - And yet again with the hand trowel, don't go for the cheap ones because they will bend and break within five minutes of you using them. I've been through my fair share of them since I've been gardening, but have found the best one now, which I'm recommending to you. Again, it's a **Burgon & Ball and is their Transplanter Trowel.** It's great because it has measurements down the blade. It costs about £10 as well.

Secateurs - Now this is a tricky one, firstly the spelling is a bugger and I just write "snippy snaps", and secondly make sure you look after them because they will go rusty very quickly and then they just don't work properly.

Don't buy any with a visible spring between the handles, because the spring always falls out and then you have to manually move the handle back and forth.

Once the spring has fallen out, it won't fit back in again. So, don't go for the cheap ones. Also look for how the blades are locked shut for safety. Some have a latch, which I personally find a pain because you're usually wearing gardening gloves and have to remove your gloves every time you want to lock them. I prefer the snippy snaps that have the knob on top that you slide back and forth. It's much easier and simpler to use.

The blades are also different shapes, some are short and stumpy, and some are long and thin. I prefer the blades that go to a point at the end as they are more precise when pruning your gooseberry bushes. There are lots to choose from, but I would personally recommend **Wolf Garden Bypass Secateurs** which cost about £20. Yes I know it's a lot, but they will last and have a ten year guarantee.

. . .

Gloves - Now you may think this is an easy decision to make, but again it's down to your own personal preference. I've tried on many gloves in my time gardening and usually in a season go through about five pairs. The holes always end up on my left glove, at the end of the glove where my thumb and index finger are. That's because I hold the hand fork or trowel with my right hand and pick up the weeds with my left hand. I need lots of "give" in my gloves so the heavy duty ones are no good as they don't give your fingers any flexibility. They are great if you're removing brambles though, but if the thorns are large enough, they will still poke through. Also don't bother with the gloves that say they can be washed in the washing machine. If you do as much gardening as I think you will be doing, then it's a pointless exercise. I don't want soil clogging up my pipes, thank you very much.

When choosing gloves, go and try them all on. Make sure they're the right size.

The measurements on the back of the packets are never correct, so use that just as a guide only and not as a rule. There are also so many colours to choose from, so take your pick. Think about what you want from them; if you need your fingers to bend easily then go for something softer. They vary in price, but can cost anywhere between £5 - £10. When you find some that you really like and work for you, then go and buy a few extra pairs. They won't expire or go mouldy if you don't use them straight away. They can sit in your shed over winter, and will be there ready for you to use the following season.

EXTRAS TO THINK ABOUT GETTING

Knee pads - Some people get a soft cushioned kneeler, but personally I prefer knee pads that you attach to your knees. The pads are better, because they're always where you need them to be. If you've got a kneeler, whenever you move to another part of your garden you have to remember to take it with you. Also if it's a bit on the windy side then the kneeler could go for a bit of a wander. Kneelers can be bought very cheaply for just a few pounds, but pads cost you a little more. Mine are from Town and Country and cost about £9, but are worth every penny. They have a couple of velcro straps that you attach together round the back of your knee, and so are very easy to put on and take off. I've had my knee pads for about four years now and they've not worn out yet. They were pink, but are now more of a mud colour.

Flexi Tub - A Flexi Tub is a flexible plastic bucket with handles. They are very useful for carrying around your vegetable plot because they are very lightweight but are sturdy enough for you to put any garden rubbish in. Because Flexi Tubs are smaller than a wheelbarrow, they are much easier to store away when you're not using them. They come in a variety of sizes and colours, so choose what ever one you want. If you want to have a colour scheme going with your wellingtons, gloves, knee pads and Flexi tub, then by all means do. It's difficult to put a price on a Flexi Tub, as it depends what size you want to buy. But they're available in most DIY stores and garden centres.

Wellington Boots - You don't have to have Wellingtons, but just make sure you put aside some suitable footwear for the garden. Remember, it will get wet and muddy when you're gardening, so I prefer to wear my Wellingtons. Invest in a good thick pair of socks as well, as toes can get cold in Wellingtons. I have purple Hunter Wellies. They are expensive, but I use mine everyday, so get my money's worth out of them.

Petrol Strimmer - You'll only need one of these if you have an allotment (or a really huge garden). I use mine on the allotment all the time to cut the grass. It's much easier than going around with a pair of shears. A decent petrol strimmer will cost you a little over £100. Yes, I know it seems a lot of money, but if you take care of it then it will last you for years and years. I've only bought one and it's still going after about ten years. Don't be tempted to get a cordless strimmer. Yes they are much, much cheaper, but the battery has to charge for about 8 hours before you can use it each time, and the power of the strimmer, even when the battery is fully charged, is frankly pathetic. You'll regret it as soon as you buy it.

What is the difference between a **strimmer** and a **brushcutter**? A **strimmer** has a nylon line and is suitable for strimming grass and other light vegetation. A **brushcutter** has both a metal blade and a nylon line and is suitable for cutting down brambles and other thick vegetation. Brushcutters are a lot more expensive.

. . .

Music - If you like to listen to nature as you garden, then don't worry about this little extra. But, if like me, you like to listen to music while you work in the garden, then a very good pair of headphones and a good upbeat music play list is a must. If you like to listen to the cricket scores, then maybe a radio is more for you, but I'll leave this specific one for you to figure out for yourself.

GARDEN OR ALLOTMENT?

This depends firstly on how much are you planning on growing. Will it all fit in the area you are willing to set aside of your garden for a vegetable patch? How far away is the nearest allotment site to you?

I'll go through a few options for you to think about before you decide where the best place is for you.

The Garden

Is your garden large enough? If you only have a very small garden and you have a family with/or are hoping to have children, will they need to play in the garden? The garden is a very important place to socialise with family and friends, and on hot summer days (yes we do get those in the UK), you yourself may want to sit and relax in your garden with a cool drink, and gaze in wonderment at the domain you have created.

A vegetable patch can be a very messy place and not as peaceful as a flower bed.

If you do have your vegetable plot in your garden, you can pop in and out dodging the rain showers (we gets *lots* of those in the UK), and if you only have half an hour to spare in the garden, it's much easier to do something in the garden than go to the allotment for such a short time. Another great thing about having your plot in the garden is that you can pick some produce for dinner and cook it immediately. All your produce will then be so fresh and flavoursome. Herbs are on hand all the time, and you don't have to cart your tools down with you to the allotment every time.

Plus, at home you have access to your own loo, which for me is very important (I'm not a fan of Portaloos).

The Allotment

With an allotment you have so much more space, and even if you start off with a small plot, you can usually get another one, or move to a larger plot. There are also the other amazing plot holders that you meet while you're down there.

The sense of community is brilliant. You'll find some real characters as well. An allotment site is full of people from all walks of life, all ages, and you're all down on the site for exactly the same reason.

People are there to give you advice and please, always ask for help, because you can guarantee that if you've got a problem with something, someone will know how to help. Ask if they have a committee and how you can join. It usually only costs a few pounds, but they'll hopefully then keep you updated with any events that are going on.

If you have an entire day to yourself, then you can escape from the rat race. Take a packed lunch, plenty of fluids and make a day of it on your plot.

You'll come back hot, dirty, and usually smelly, but you'll feel a real sense of achievement.

Then you can get in the bath and soak away all those aches and pains.

WHAT IS AN ALLOTMENT?

A Brief History

An allotment is a typically British invention and they have been around for hundreds of years. The allotments that we know and love today were started just after the 1900s, but came into full use just after WW1. Allotments were then used to help returning servicemen recover from the traumas of war. But during WW2, allotments came into their own as food rationing came in and any spare scrap of land was turned over to the cultivation of fruits and vegetables.

Dig for Victory was the slogan, and boy did the British dig in earnest.

As the decades came and went the number of allotment plots rose and fell. Some decades saw a surge in people wanting them, like the 1970s, with the TV series *The Good Life*, but also there were a wave of strikes and unemployment was very high. People needed to do what they could to survive. But in the 2000s the take-up was fairly low. I got my first plot in 2005, and the site I was on was barely half full. A few years later there was a resurgence and now the plot is full and we have a waiting list.

An Allotment site

This is how allotment sites work in the UK, other countries are different. An allotment site is a large piece of land (the site) and the land is divided up into lots of smaller pieces of land (the plots). Most of the plots are roughly the same size, but some plots are smaller and other plots are larger. Usually the site is run by the local authority, but some are self-managed.

You pay an annual rent for your allotment plot. This varies from area to area, so check this out before you apply for a plot.

For the council run sites, you pay your rent straight to the council. For the self-managed sites you pay your rent directly to the committee on that site.

You have your plot for an entire year, and then can renew the following year. You keep the same plot (unless you decide to move). Each site has different rules about sheds and other structures so please check out all the rules beforehand.

Also watch out for water charges, sometimes these are included in the rent, and other times they are not.

HOW TO GET AN ALLOTMENT

This varies from country to country, but this is how it works in the UK. Whether you are wanting to be on a local authority or a self-managed site, the best place to start is to contact your local authority. They will point you in the right direction, or they should be able to.

Most sites will have a waiting list, some are months long and others are years. It just depends on where you live. Ask where all the sites are in your borough and what the waiting lists are like on each one.

If there are self-managed sites in your borough the local authority should be able to give you the person to contact.

When choosing the site you want to be on, look at whether there is vehicle access. Some small sites don't have this, so you'd have to carry everything some distance.

Also, make sure your site has water taps. I know this may seem obvious, but some sites don't have mains water and this is tricky when you want to water your seedlings.

A shed is not essential, and there may be restrictions on sizes of structures, so if you are wanting to have a greenhouse then you must check this out.

There could also be restrictions on what you are allowed to grow. Obviously you can't grow anything illegal, but sometimes people like to grow bamboo. This spreads under the ground, so could end up on a neighbouring plot, or sometimes you're not allowed to grow trees above a certain height, so it's worth checking any restrictions out as well.

Look around each site before you decide which one is best for you. Check out the soil on each one. There are six types of soil: **clay, sandy, silty, peaty, chalky and loamy.**

Clay soil is very claggy, difficult to dig and sticks together in large clumps. It does retain water, but sets very hard when it dried out and doesn't let the water drain through. Adding lots of well rotten horse manure or other organic matter to clay soil helps break up the large lumps.

Sandy and **silty** soils are very similar, in that they are very fine. If you get a handful of either of these and squeeze it together they don't form a mass. They don't hold water at all, but let the water drain through very easily. Adding manure to these soils will help bind the fine soil together.

Peaty soil is very dark in colour and very soft. It absorbs water very easily, but it's very rich and many plants don't like this. In the summer it goes very dry and can become a fire hazard.

Chalky soil is not good for many plants as it stops the plants from absorbing the necessary water they need. As you dig the soil, you'll find chunks of white chalk in the soil, and you will also find a white layer coating the surface of the soil. Manure is also useful in improving chalky soil as well, because it will allow the water to absorb into it.

Loamy soil is the best, and if you can find this then you've hit the jackpot. On the surface of the soil it looks a mid-brown in colour, and is fairly fine. If you grab a handful of it and squeeze it together, then it will form a mass. But if you push it with a finger it will fall apart again. There should also be some small stones in the soil to help with drainage.

Soils can always be improved by using manure and other organic matter, but if you start of with fairly decent soil, then you're on to a winner. When looking at an allotment site, don't be afraid to get your hands dirty. Look at other people's plots on the site and see what their soil looks like.

Once you have chosen the site that is best for you, then you need to decide which plot to have on that site.

Don't go for anything too large to start with.

The plot you choose will most probably be overgrown. You'll have to clear it before you even start planting.

Once you've chosen the plot you want then let your local authority contact or self-managed site contact know and then they'll let you know when you can start digging.

PREPARING YOUR GROWING AREA

Now that you have decided where you're going to grow your vegetables, you need to get the ground prepared. I will go through a few suggestions which I hope will help you.

Raised beds are great. Yes they are expensive, but if they're built properly then they can last for about 20 years, if not longer. They can be built to whatever size you want and as tall as you want.

The bed can be as long as you want, but make sure that the bed is no wider than four foot. The reason for this is that most people can only comfortably stretch about two foot. So if the bed is wider than four foot then you can't reach the centre.

You can either make the raised beds yourself by using Wickes Jumbo Garden Sleepers or can get them pre-made and put them together yourself. I would recommend Woodblocx as they are excellent. When putting the beds together with these, it's like building with large wooden Lego bricks.

If using raised beds you don't have to dig any of the soil up, just place the raised beds directly on the grass.

Once you have constructed your raised bed, then place a thick layer of flattened cardboard boxes in the bottom, this will stop the grass from growing up. On top of the cardboard place a thick layer of wood chips.

If you know someone who is a tree surgeon then I'm sure you can get some for free, as they usually have to pay to dispose of them and you'll be doing them a favour.

Then fill the remainder of the bed up with a mixture of well rotted mature (which, again, you can usually get free from a stables), soil and some small stones. The small stones will help with drainage.

Check the soil before you buy, as it may be full of all sorts of rubbish. Before you buy some small stones check what is in the soil. If there are plenty of small stones in the soil already, then don't worry about adding any more.

Fill the bed to the very top, because it will eventually settle and the level of the soil will drop quite considerably.

Ground Beds are great as well. They don't cost anything, unlike the raised beds, which is very important. You can change the sizes of them as often as you like. Again, when digging your ground beds, make sure that they're no wider than four foot, but as long as you like.

Before you start digging, mark out the area that you are going to use for your ground beds. Cover the entire area with dark thick plastic and secure down. Leave the plastic down for about a month.

After about a month, turn back a small amount of plastic and you'll find that the grass and weeds below have turned brown. The soil should still be soft, and this will make it easy to dig.

Push your large fork into the ground as far as you can and pull it back. This will open up the ground. Pull the fork out and push the fork in again, but just behind of where you have previously dug, and then pull back again. Keep doing this, as it will open up the soil and loosen it up.

Once you have opened up a good amount of the soil, then get down on your hands and knees (this is where your knee pads will come in handy), and use your small fork to remove the grass and weeds.

Sorting out the soil this way is much easier, and there is no heavy lifting and turning over of soil. The weeds and grass remain on the surface of the soil, and are easy for you to remove.

Once you have done one bed, then create a little path between each bed. These are necessary as you will need to be able to walk between each bed. You can either let these paths become grass again, but doing this means a lot of upkeep. Or you can always cover your paths with weed suppressant fabric and wood chips. The paths will then stay very neat and tidy and are very low maintenance.

Keep moving the thick plastic back until you have dug all the beds you want.

Once you have all your beds prepared, then put a thick layer (about 2 inches thick) of well rotted horse manure. Spread it on the top of each bed and give a light forking in to the soil. Well rotted manure is dark brown/black in colour and stables are usually desperate for people to take it away free of charge.

Manure is gardeners' gold, so try and find a local source.

DIFFERENT TYPES OF WEEDS

There are many different types of weeds you are likely to get. The way to eradicate weeds is to get them out as soon as possible. Don't let them go to seed, otherwise you'll be inundated the following year.

What are Perennial weeds? Perennials are plants that have a life cycle of more that one year, and therefore come back year after year. The most likely perennial weeds you'll come across are: ground elder, horsetail, bindweed, and dandelions. I hope you never come across knotweed which is a very invasive weed and grows incredibly fast and is very hard to get rid of.

What are Annual weeds? Annual weeds have a life cycle of only one year. The most likely ones you are going to come across are: chick-weed, nettles, shepherd's purse and groundsel.

Of course there are many more out there that you may come across, but some you may never see at all, like couch grass and thistles.

All of these weeds tend to die back during the winter months and then, as soon as the weather gets warm again, they come into full growth. The best way to rid your growing area of weeds is to completely remove any weeds and take them as far away as possible. Don't even be tempted to put bindweed, nettles or any flowering weeds, or weeds with seed heads, on your compost heap, as they will just take root and spread. Personally, I would take any weeds to the garden waste area of your local recycling centre.

If you spend a year picking out every weed as soon it appears then the following year you'll have far fewer weeds. You may feel like you're spending your entire growing season on your knees, but it'll be worth it in the end.

I hope I have inspired you and you will now start planning what you would like to grow this year. Whether it's your first attempt at growing, or you've been growing for many years. I hope you try at least one new fruit or vegetable this year that you've never tried before. Remember you don't have to grow everything from seed, just pop down to your local garden centre and see what takes your fancy.

The joy that you'll get from eating your fresh produce is second to none. The flavour of freshly harvested produce is amazing. I hope this information helps you on your way to growing your own fruit and vegetables. So let's take this journey together and discover the joys of gardening.

- If you have any questions please ask via my blog: https://clairesallotment.com
- Or Claire's Allotment YouTube videos: https://www.youtube.com/user/clairesallotment/
- Or clairesallotment@gmail.com

Let's get started...

BEETROOT

INTRODUCTION

We have been growing beetroots since the Ancient Greek times, back in 300 BC. But these beetroots were long and thin, a bit like a carrot. The Ancients Greeks only ate the leaves and not the roots of the beetroot. But they didn't throw away the root, they were offered to the sun god Apollo. The leaves were also used to dress wounds, and were also thought to prolong life. So therefore they were very highly sought after and were very important.

When the Romans arrived, they used to eat the roots as well, but these were only for medicinal purposed.

It was thought they would cure a fever, but they were also used as a laxative!

Round beetroots didn't arrive until 16th and 17th century in Europe, but took a couple of hundred years to spread across the whole of Europe and become commonplace in most countries.

Beetroots were very popular during Victorian times, as they

brought colour to the bland looking foods and, because of their sweet flavour, they were used in many desserts.

Due to rationing during the second world war, beetroot were pickled and were preserved in sterilised jars.

These days, we have a wonderful array of all sorts of different shapes and colours of beetroot, and they are very easy to grow in most climates across the world.

Now we eat the entire beetroot plant. From the leaves, which are great harvested young and used in salads, to mature leaves that can be sliced thinly and used in a stir fry.

The root part of the beetroot, can either harvested when they are small, or left in the soil until they are much larger. Beetroots are ready to eat whatever their size.

In the UK we call them beetroot, but in North America they're either called beets, table beets, garden beets, red beets or golden beets. Beetroots are now used in many countries around the work and, as a result, there are many wonderful dishes out there for you to explore.

Beetroots are full of all sorts of vitamins and minerals from calcium, iron, vitamins, A & C, folic acid, fibre, manganese and potassium.

DIFFERENT TYPES OF BEETROOT

Beetroot comes in two types: Mono-germ and Multi-germ. These are rather odd words, so let me explain them both in a little more detail.

Mono-germ seeds

Mono-germ seeds have only 1 embryo in them, therefore one seed will only grow one plant. If you are growing a mono-germ type of beetroot, you are less likely to have to thin out your seedlings as they grow.

When sowing your seeds, you should space them 3 inches apart from each other in the soil, and that way they will have enough room to grow.

The varieties of mono-germ beetroots I would recommend are either

Moneta, which are round and deep red in colour, or if you prefer long beetroot, then I would recommend Monorubra, which are long and dark pink.

Multi-germ seeds

Multi-germ seeds have either 2 or 3 embryos in each seed, so therefore you could get 3 plants growing from one seed. Depending on how many seeds you grow, you may have thin them out, which will allow plenty of room for the beetroots to swell up. When your beetroots grow close together this is called "clustering". If you are growing the multi-germ beetroots, I would recommend you grow either Boltardy, which are deep pink and round, Burpees Golden, which are orange on the outside and yellow on the inside, or Chioggia, which are deep pink on the outside, but have pink and white concentric circles on the inside.

Whichever beetroots you decide to grow, they all need to be grown and looked after in the same way. Beetroot have a very earthy flavour to them, and eating freshly cooked beetroot has so much more flavour that the tasteless, vinegar soaked ones you buy in a jar.

WHEN TO SOW YOUR BEETROOT SEEDS

Whether you are growing mono-germ or multi-germ beetroot seeds, they all can be sown at the same time.

The times I'm giving are for the southern part of the UK, so if your climate is warmer, then you can sow them a little sooner, but if your climate is cooler you'll need to sow your seeds a little later.

I sow my beetroot seeds outside in the soil from the middle of April, but you can continue to sow them all the way through to the end of June.

Sow your beetroot seeds "in succession", which means sow some in the middle of April, and then some more a month later. You can keep doing this until the end of June. That way you'll be harvesting them from Summer all the way through to the end of autumn.

However, if you want to get an early crop of beetroot, then you can sow them in the soil in early March. But you must protect your growing seedlings from the cold weather and frost. You can do this by putting a protective cloche over the top of your seeds. The cloche will hold in the heat, and prevent the frost from getting to the seeds underneath. The cloche can be removed during the day from the middle of April, but must be put back over the seedlings at night. You can remove the cloche completely at the end of April.

HOW TO SOW YOUR BEETROOT SEEDS

Beetroot seeds are quite large, round and knobbly. They look like they're all shrivelled up and won't germinate, but however weird they might look, they will germinate if sown correctly.

> Before you sow your beetroot seeds, make sure you dig over the soil to remove any weeds and large stones. If there are a few small stones in the soil, this will help with drainage.

Break down any large lumps of soil, and add in some well rotten manure, mixing it it very well.

Beetroots like free draining soil so, if you have heavy clay soil, add a good amount of sand and well rotten manure to the soil helps break up the clay clods. The sand will also help with drainage.

If you are growing the long beetroots, then they will need to be able to push through the soil. If there are too many obstacles in the way, like stones or large clumps of soil, you'll end up with some very bizarre shaped vegetables.

Once you have thoroughly dug and weeded the soil, you'll need to rake the soil to make it smooth and level. Raking the soil will also help remove any large stones and lumps of soil.

Now you are ready to start sowing.

I usually grow my beetroots in straight lines. This makes weeding and harvest them much easier. The best way to make a straight line is by using a piece of thin garden rope. Tie each end of the rope to a short metal pole, because you'll need to push the poles into the soil, and anything other than metal will be too fragile, and will break.

Decide where you want the line of beetroot to start, and push one of the poles into the soil, then unravel the rope, and push the other pole into the soil at the end of the line.

Once you have your line marked out, you need to make a shallow trough, about 1 inch deep, all along the line. Stay as close to the rope as you can.

Use a watering can, without the rose attachment. Water in the trough and wait for the water to soak all the way through the soil before you sow your seeds.

> Watering the trough helps the seeds to germinate a little sooner because, once they are sown, they are immediately in contact with some damp soil.

Once the water has completely soaked through, then you can start to sow your seeds. Sow 1 or 2 beetroot seeds every 3 inches all the way along the trough.

> If you sow your beetroot seeds too close together, they will need thinning out as they grow, and you will waste lots of valuable seeds.

The germination rate for beetroot seeds is very good, so there is no need to overcrowd them when you sow the seeds.

When you have sown your beetroot seeds, very carefully cover them over with soil. Gently pat the soil down, and then label one end of the line, so you know what is growing, making sure you write on the label which variety you have just sown as well. Also put a stick at the other end of the line, then you know where your line begins and ends.

You should start to see the first leaves appear above the soil in about 2 weeks. Water a couple of times a week, using a watering can, with a rose attachment on the end. Water the top of the soil and allow the water to soak through the soil to the seeds.

Don't overwater as the seeds will rot. If you have had a heavy downpour, then you will not need to water your seeds.

GROWING BEETROOTS IN RAISED BEDS AND CONTAINERS

All varieties of beetroots will grow very well in raised beds and container.

If you have a raised bed, put a layer of wood chips in the base, and then fill with a mixture of soil, manure and a little ballast. Make sure the ballast doesn't have any cement in it. Fill your raised bed to the very top and leave it to settle for a week before sowing your seeds.

If you have a container, fill the base with some large stone, bricks, or broken terracotta. Then fill the container with a mixture of soil, manure and a little ballast.

Adding the ballast helps with drainage. Gently press the contents down and then you can start to sow straight away.

Beetroots have a long tap root that goes down into the soil to find water, but the roots don't spread out much. If you are growing beetroot in a shallow container or raised bed, then I would suggest you grow a round beetroot rather than a long beetroot. The variety I would suggest are Red Hawk F1, which are fast growing, very sweet and perfect when harvested as baby beetroot.

If you have a deep raised beds or containers, then you can grow any variety you like.

Make sure that there are adequate drainage holes in the bottom on your raised beds or containers. If beetroot seeds get wet, and stay wet for too long, they will rot.

Sow the seeds in the same way as you would in the open ground and, as they grow, look after them in the same way.

THE FIRST LEAVES

Beetroot leaves are very easy to see. They have a bright red stem and a long thin green leaf. You'll see two oval leaves appear first, then more leaves will come from the centre of the plant. The first leaves will grow a little more, but still stay small, and will always be oval.

After a while, they will shrivel and disappear. This is quite normal, so don't worry.

The rest of the leaves will also be oval to start with, but will then become more jagged round the outside as they grow. They will grow with the plant, and will get to about 6 inches long, and 4 inches wide.

Thinning out your beetroot seedlings

Sometimes you won't need to do this because, as your seeds germinate, they may have plenty of room around them to grow.

If however, if they are growing too close to each other, and some of your beetroots are stopping the other beetroots around them from swelling up properly, then you will have to thin your seedlings out.

Thinning out must be done with great care, as you do not want to disturb the roots of the seedlings that you are leaving in.

> The best way to thin your beetroots out is by getting down on your hands and knees and going along the line very carefully. If you have a group, or cluster of seedlings growing together, you will need to remove all but the strongest seedlings.

Water the soil first to make it much easier to carefully pull out the unwanted seedlings. Using your thumb and forefinger, pinch hold of a seedling you want to pull out, and then slowly and carefully remove the seedling. The unwanted seedlings can then go in the compost heap.

Make sure that any disturbed soil is put back and once you have finished thinning out your entire row, water again.

HOW TO LOOK AFTER YOUR BEETROOT AS THEY GROW

Beetroot are very easy to look after, they don't need a huge amount of attention to be honest. There are just a few things you need to remember to do.

Weeding

Make sure your plants are kept weed free. Weeds grow very fast, and if you don't weed regularly the weeds will take over, suffocate your beetroot seedlings, and they won't grow. Once a week meticulously go along your line of beetroot, and remove any weeds that you see trying to grow. If the weeds are very small, you will be able to remove them very easily. The sooner you pull the weeds out the better.

> If you meticulously weed every week, then the weeds will be very small and won't have gone to seed, therefore reducing the likelihood of further weeds growing later on.

Water

As with most other plants, water is very important to helping your plants grow well. But it must be the right amount of water. Too little water and your beetroots will get very woody. Woody means that the inside of the beetroot is very hard and stringy. You can't eat a woody beetroot, it feels like you're eating tree bark, hence the name.

> Too much water and your beetroots will split and crack. The sudden onset of a load of water is absorbed by the roots and because the beetroot swells very quickly. The skin of the beetroot can't cope with the sudden growth, so it splits. Splits can lead to infection getting into the flesh and can rot the plant.

You need to make sure that you get the watering right. I would suggest that when your plants are very small, water twice a week, but make sure you don't over water them. Using a watering can, with a rose attachment on the end of the pouring spout, water a little, and wait for the water to soak into the soil. If you are due a heavy downpour, then don't water.

When your plants get a little larger you can water them a little more, but still only twice a week. Even in a heatwave they will only need watering twice a week, but as they grow they will need a little more watering.

Feeding

From early June onwards, every time you water you beetroots, feed them at the same time. I use Shropshire Seaweed Fertiliser. You need to add a very small amount of this to the water, the instructions are on the bottle. You can buy Shropshire Seaweed Fertiliser very easily online. I swear by this, and have been using it for many years.

If you make sure you look after your beetroots as they grow, then they will reward you with an excellent crop.

Pests and diseases

There aren't many pests and diseases that can effect your beetroot crop. But here are some that you may come across:

Black leg

This can happen to seedlings if the seeds are sown too close together and the seeds get waterlogged.

The best way to prevent this from happening, is to sow your seedling very thinly, spacing them at least 3 inches apart from each other. Watch your local weather forecast, and if heavy rain is due, then you won't need to water. As long as you have dug the soil well, then the rain should trickle through the soil and the seeds won't sit in the wet for too long.

If you do get black leg, then remove the diseased plants immediately.

Bolting

This is when your plants send out a tall seed shoot from the centre of the plant. This is the plant's way of reproducing. Once a plant starts to bolt, your need to cut off the shoot and harvest the beetroot immediately. If you leave the beetroot in the soil any longer, the centre will go woody, and therefore the beetroot will become inedible.

To help minimise your plants from bolting, make sure you water them regularly. If your plants get very dry on a regular basis, this will make them bolt.

You can buy bolt resistant varieties, "Boltardy" or "Rubidus" which are very good varieties to try.

Fanging

This is sometimes called "forking". This happens when the bulb of your beetroots hits a stone or a large solid object and the bulb splits and then continues to grow. Instead of harvesting a lovely long or round beetroot, your could harvest one that is a very bizarre shape.

To stop your beetroot from "fanging", make sure that you remove any large stone and objects from the soil.

WHEN TO HARVEST YOUR BEETROOT

Beetroot are ready when ever you are. You don't have to wait for them to ripen. The longer you leave them in the soil, the larger the roots will swell. It's up to you as to whether you want to harvest your beetroot when they are small, medium, or large.

You can start to harvest any small beetroot from the middle of June. If some of your crop are growing too close together, then I would suggest carefully pull up some of the small ones, to allow the others more space to grow.

Check your beetroots every couple of weeks and harvest any others that you want.

You should harvest the last of your beetroot by the end of October. If a light frost is forecast, then cover your crop up with a cloche. Frost will stop your beetroot from growing anymore, but also the day time temperatures in October are getting cold, so your beetroots won't grow any more.

How to harvest your beetroot

Harvesting your beetroot is very easy. Hold all the leaves of one beetroot plant at the base, where the leaves join the beetroot, and pull upwards. The beetroot should come out easily. Then fill in the hole with some soil, and water.

The first beetroots you harvest will be fairly small, but still very tasty. Then check every couple of weeks, and harvest a few more. If you harvest every couple of weeks, it'll give the beetroots still left in the ground more time to swell.

This way you'll have a great supply throughout the summer. Make sure that your last beetroots are harvested by the end of October.

Once the temperature starts to drop, and the threat of frost comes to your area, you'll find that your beetroots won't grow any more. If you are leaving your beetroots in the soil into November, make sure you cover them with a cloche so they stay warmer. This will also stop the slugs and snails from getting to them because the soil isn't really wet.

I have tried overwintering some beetroots before, but found the plants went to seed and then woody. They were inedible and I had to put them on the compost heap.

HOW TO STORE YOUR BEETROOT

There are many different ways of storing beetroot.

In the shops beetroot usually comes either sliced or whole in jars, and are preserved in sweet vinegar. I love both these ingredients separately, but together not at all. I find that the vinegar makes the beetroot very sharp, where beetroot is naturally sweet.

Preserving

If you like beetroot preserved in sweet vinegar then it is very easy to do at home, and store them in a sterilised glass jar.

- Firstly wash your raw beetroots, and remove the stems and the leaves. Wrap each beetroot individually in foil, and roast in the oven until they are tender. This should take about and hour to an hour and a half.
- Now you can get the preserving liquid ready.
- In a large saucepan, put in your spices. You can use whatever spices you like, but I would recommend using peppercorns, mustard seeds, coriander seeds, bay leaves

and a couple of whole dried chillies. You can use as much or as little of these as you like.

- Over a low heat, roast all these spices in a dry saucepan for a couple of minutes, until they start to release their aroma.
- Once the spices start to release their aroma, then you need to add some white wine vinegar to the saucepan. You'll need enough vinegar to fill your jars. Always add little extra vinegar as some will evaporate.
- Add a little soft brown sugar to the vinegar mixture and stir it all together, making sure the sugar dissolves completely.
- Bring the vinegar to the boil, and boil gently for 5 minutes.
- Once your beetroot are cooked, remove the skins, cut into slices, and put in your sterile jar. Pour the vinegar mixture over the top of the beetroot, making sure you cover all the beetroot, and seal the jar.
- Once you have sealed the beetroot and vinegar in a sterilised glass jar, you'll need to leave it to infuse for at least a couple of weeks before using, or longer if you have the patience. Once the jar has been opened, it must be kept in the fridge and eaten within 6 weeks. An unopened jar will keep for 6 months to a year.

Freezing

Another way to preserve your beetroots is to freeze them in the deep freeze. Before you freeze them, you will need to boil them until they are tender. How long this will take, depends on the size of your beetroots.

- Remove the leaves, and clean off any soil off the beetroots. Using a large saucepan, fill two thirds full with cold water. Place the beetroots in the water, and bring to the boil. Small beetroots will take about 10 minutes, but larger beetroots about 30 minutes. It's best to make sure that all the beetroots in the saucepan are approximately the same size.

- You will know when the beetroots are cooked, because you can insert a knife in them easily.
- Allow the beetroots to cool completely in the water, and then peel off the beetroot skins, the skins will come of very easily. Place the beetroots in a plastic box and put in the freezer.
- If you then want some beetroot with your dinner, just take out what you need from the freezer and allow to defrost at room temperature for about an hour or so.
- They will keep perfectly in the freezer for up to 1 year.

In wooden crates

If you have a cool garage or shed then, once you've harvested your crop, remove the leaves and lay your beetroots in a single layer in wooden crates. Cover your beetroots with fresh multi purpose compost. Only use fresh compost because it is sterile.

Only store perfect beetroot, and if you find any damaged ones, make sure you use them straight away.

Check your beetroots once a week for signs incase any of them are going bad, and if any are, remove and eat them straight away.

Your beetroots should store perfectly well like this until early spring the following year.

BEETROOT RECIPE

Beetroots are a very versatile vegetable. They can be used in cakes, soups, salads, dips, jellies, pies, or just eaten on their own as a vegetable accompanying a main course. They can be boiled, roast, sautéed or fried.

Because they are naturally sweet they are perfect in either savoury or sweet dishes. They can either be served hot, warm, or cold.

I like to roast my beetroots, as I always feel that roasting vegetables brings out their natural sugars and their flavour becomes more intense. But please feel free to try whatever recipes that inspire you.

Roasted beetroots are the perfect accompaniment to oven roasted chicken legs, served with a little green salad of mixed leaves. Add in some baby beetroot leaves to the salad to bring the dish together and maybe add some parmesan shavings on top of the salad as well.

Roasted Beetroots

Ingredients

- 6 medium sized beetroots, cleaned, with the leaves and small roots removed, but keep the skins on
- 4 fl oz of good olive oil
- Salt and pepper, a good pinch of each
- 1 lemon, zest and juice

Method

1. Set the oven to Gas mark 4/180C/360F
2. Remove the leaves and small roots from the beetroots, but make sure you keep the skins on. Then give the beetroot a good wash and pat dry.
3. Wrap each beetroot loosely in kitchen foil, and place on a backing tray.
4. Place the tray on the shelf in the centre of the oven and roast for about 1-1.5 hours. The larger the beetroot are, the longer they will take to cook. You will know when they are cooked, because you will be able to push a knife into the beetroot very easily.
5. Once the beetroot are cooked, remove from the oven. Open up the foil, and leave to cool for about 30 minutes.
6. While the beetroots are cooling, you can make the vinaigrette.
7. In a large bowl, add the grated lemon zest, and the juice of the lemon. Add a good pinch of salt and pepper, and then slowly whisk in the olive oil.
8. When the beetroots are cool enough for you to handle, remove the skins of the beetroot, and cut them into one and a half inch cubes.
9. Once you have cut up all the beetroots, add them into the

bowl with the vinaigrette and give everything a good stir. Because the beetroots are still warm, they will absorb the vinaigrette very well.

10. Leave for the flavours to infuse for about 15 minutes before serving.

BROAD BEANS

INTRODUCTION

Broad beans have many names, it all depends where you live. In the UK we refer to them as Broad beans, but in other countries they are referred to as java beans, fava beans, faba beans, field beans, bell beans or tic beans.

They are grown all over the world from China, Egypt, Luxembourg, Spain, and all the way to the Sudan. They are a staple part of many dishes in these countries.

Broad beans are often overlooked, but freshly cooked young broad beans are sweet and delicious.

I hope to convince you that they are a vegetable worth growing. They are very easy to grow, and don't take up much space, and they also don't need a huge amount of looking after.

If you are new to gardening, then broad beans are the perfect place to start. They are usually the first seeds to be sown, which always means that Spring is not far away. The germination rate is very good, and they can be sown either straight out into the soil, or started off early in a greenhouse or cold frame.

Broad beans are rich in vitamin C, fibre, and iron, as well as many other vitamins and minerals. They can help boost your immune system, and improve your sleep.

The Egyptians, Romans and Greeks all cultivated broad beans, and even now, when they harvest the year's crop, it is a cause for celebration. Some of the freshly harvested beans are eaten straight away, but much of the harvest gets dried and used over the winter months in casseroles.

DIFFERENT TYPES OF BROAD BEANS

There are two different types of broad beans. One is the autumn and spring sowing variety, and the other is the dwarf variety. They both grow in exactly the same way, but their sowing times are slightly different.

Autumn and spring types

Depending on where you live, depends whether you can sow your broad bean seeds in either the autumn and the spring, or just in the spring.

If you have free draining soil, and live in the south of the UK, or in a slightly warmer climate, then you can sow your broad beans in October or November. But you must remember to sow them in a sheltered place in the garden, and cover them with a fleece when the weather is cold.

However, if you live in a cold climate, or have clay soil, then you must wait until March or April to sow your broad bean seeds.

Both autumn and spring types of broad beans will grow to about 3 feet high, and are usually self supporting, so you shouldn't need to make a frame to attach your plants to. But if your broad beans are growing in an exposed area, then you may well have to support them.

There is more information about supporting your broad bean plants later in the book.

The varieties of the autumn and spring types I like to grow are "**Aguadulce**", as I find you get a really substantial crop. They produce very flavoursome beans, and they are also cold tolerant. So you can sow them a little earlier, or if you have a late cold snap the plants are unaffected by it.

"**Bunyards Exhibition**" are also very good, and I would recommend these as well. They are a heavy cropper, and the pods are very long and packed full of beans. They are a popular choice.

Dwarf types

If space is limited, or you live in a very exposed area, then you may well be better off growing a dwarf type of broad bean. These will grow to a height of about 18 inches, and again are self supporting. These are best sown in the spring, so March and April is perfect.

The dwarf variety I would recommend you try is "**The Sutton**" as they are ideal for growing if space is limited. They are also a good cropper. The pods are small, but packed full of beans. Also "**Robin Hood,**" which is also another good dwarf variety you may wish to try. You will get 4-6 beans per pod and they are very compact plants.

I have sown both dwarf, and the standard types of broad beans, and sown in autumn and in spring.

I found that the germination rate, if I planted in the spring, was much better. If I sowed my broad bean seeds in the autumn, many of them didn't germinate at all.

WHEN TO SOW YOUR BROAD BEANS

Broad beans can either be sown in the autumn (October or November) or the spring (March or April).

The advantage of sowing them in the autumn means that they get a head start, and when the heat starts to build in the spring they are stronger.

If sowing in the autumn, they need to be sown directly in the soil in October or November. They will start to germinate before the really cold weather sets in, and then over winter they will stop growing. But once spring starts, and the warm weather comes along, then they will continue to grow again.

Make sure that when the really cold weather starts you cover your broad bean seedlings with some fleece to help protect them from the harshest weathers, as well as the birds.

If you prefer to wait until spring to sow your broad bean seeds, that's perfectly ok. They can be sown directly in the soil in March and April.

They will take about 10-14 days to germinate and will grow rapidly in the warm weather.

If March is still very cold, then you can still sow your broad bean seeds in the soil, but cover them with some fleece, or a cloche to help keep in some of the heat.

A cloche is a plastic protective covering that you can put of the seedlings as they grow. They can be either a long tunnel, or a round circular bell shape.

You don't need to go and buy an expensive cloche, the bottom half of an up-turned plastic bottle makes a perfect cloche for your growing seedlings. Place one over each seedling.

You can start your broad bean seeds off in the greenhouse. If you do this, then you can sow your seeds in January or February. As they are growing in the greenhouse, they are protected from the harsh weather, so will grow very well. You'll then be able to transplant your seedlings outside into the soil from mid March to early April. But you must make sure you acclimatise your seedlings to the outside temperatures beforehand. If you don't, the plants will go into shock, stop growing and then might even die.

To acclimatise your plants to the outside temperatures, all you have to do is to put them outside in sheltered spot in your garden during the day, and then bring them back into the greenhouse just before it gets dark.

If the weather during the day is very grim, don't put your plants outside.

Start to acclimatise your plants at least 2 weeks before you are planning on planting them outside.

HOW TO SOW YOUR BROAD BEAN SEEDS

Whichever variety you decide to grow, or whether you decide to grow them in the spring or in the autumn, your broad bean seeds need to be sown in exactly the same way.

Broad bean seeds are very large. Make sure that you check each seed before you sow them. If any of them have a small round hole in them, discard them as they are infected with the broad bean seed beetle.

If you save your own broad bean seeds to plant the following year, this tends to be a problem. But if you buy from a reputable seed company this should not be a problem. But check each seed any way.

The seed will still germinate as the beetle doesn't feed on the embryo part of the seed. But discarding the infected seeds, helps control the broad bean beetle from spreading.

Sowing in the soil

Sowing your broad bean seeds in the soil is very easy. There is no need to soak your seeds before you sow, as this weakens the outer skin of the seed, and disease may get inside the seed.

Dig over the soil very well, and fork in a good amount of well rotted manure. Make sure that your manure is well rotted, as fresh manure can bring with it pests and diseases that may ruin your crop.

Remove any large stones and break down any larger clods of soil. Broad beans like free draining soil and their roots don't like to sit in wet conditions for long.

Choose a sunny spot for them to grow, as broad beans love to be in lots of sun for as much of the day as possible.

Broad beans are usually grown in rows, so mark out a straight line using some string. Then along the string make a trough 2 inches deep, and 2 inches wide.

Put one seed every 8 inches, all the way along the trough. It doesn't matter what way up your seeds are.

When you have sown all you can in the row, fill the trough with water. Wait for the water to drain away before you cover up the seeds with soil.

Then mark each end of the line of broad beans with a stick, and put a label at one end, so you remember what you've planted.

If you want to sow more than one line of broad beans, then make sure the rows are 12 inches apart from each other.

That way your growing plants will have enough room to grow, but also be close enough to support each other as they grow tall.

Sowing in the greenhouse

If you are worried about starting your broad beans seeds off in autumn, and spring is still very cold, you can always start your broad bean seeds off in a greenhouse or cold frame.

The greenhouse or cold frame will protect your growing seedlings from the extreme weather conditions outside, as well as protecting them against any pest that will start to nibble their freshly emerging shoots.

The best way to sow your broad bean seeds is to get a 3 inch pot and fill it all the way to the top with multi purpose compost. Give the compost a gentle pat down, and then water the compost from above. Wait for the water to drain all the way through the compost before planting your broad bean seed.

You can only sow 1 broad bean seed per 3 inch pot. Place the broad bean seed on top of the compost and push it down into the compost about 2 inches. Then fill in the hole with more compost.

You'll only need to water when the compost is dry. Make sure you don't over water, as the broad bean seeds don't like to sit in really wet compost for very long.

After 10-14 days little green shoots should start to appear above the compost. Water your seedlings when the soil is dry, and always water on the top of the compost.

At this early stage in the seed's development, always water from above, then your broad bean seeds won't sit in really wet compost and rot. If your broad bean seeds rot, then the plant will die.

Keep your seedlings in the greenhouse until the middle of March, when you can then transplant them outside. But make sure you acclimatise your plants before transplanting them, as the sudden change in temperature will shock your plants, and they will either stop growing, or die.

The best way to acclimatise your plants is to place them in a shelter part of your garden during the day and then put them back in the greenhouse over night. Do this for 14 days before you transplant them outside.

Growing broad beans in raised beds or containers

Broad beans will grow very well in raised beds and large containers, but there are a few things that you have to think about before decided which type of broad beans you are going to grow.

Broad beans like the sun, so choose where you are going to put your raised beds or containers every carefully. They don't mind a little bit of shade, but make sure they're not it complete shade.

Containers

These need to be as large as you can get, I would suggest nothing smaller that 2 feet across. The depth of the container is important as well, as the roots of the broad bean plants will need to go down. With this in mind, make sure that you container is at least 1 foot deep.

Make sure there are plenty of drainage holes in the bottom of your container. Then place some broken bricks or broken terracotta in the base, these will help with drainage and also stop the drainage holes from blocking up. It will also add some weight to the container.

Fill the container with a mixture of compost and well rotted manure. Broad beans are hungry plants and need some extra feed added to the soil.

Fill the container to the very top, and then let it settle for about a week before planting your broad bean seeds or plants.

It may be best to grow the dwarf broad beans in containers, as the tall ones may make the container top heavy and it could fall over in the wind.

Raised beds

Growing broad beans in raised beds, is very easy. Make sure there is a thick layer of wood chips in the base of the raised bed, as this will help with drainage. Fill the rest of the raised bed with a mixture of compost, ballast (making sure there is no cement in it), and well rotted manure. Fill the raised bed to the very top, and then leave it to settle for at least a week before you plant your broad bean seeds or plants.

> If you have a small raised bed, then grow a dwarf variety of broad bean, but if your raised bed is fairly large and sturdy, then you can grow whatever variety you like.

The first leaves

As your broad bean seed germinates it splits into 2 parts, and the roots grow down and then a green shoot will come from the centre of the split seed.

Usually the split seed will stay below the ground, but sometimes it pokes through the soil. If this happens, don't worry.

As the plant grows, the seed halves will shrivel up and then disappear.

A thick green stem will continue to grow, and wrapped around the stem are the leaves. As the stem grows up, the leaves will uncurl from the stem and open up. The stem will continue to grow and more leaves will unravel.

As a general rule, one seed produces one stem, but sometimes you can get more than one stem per seed. If this does happen, then it's advisable to stake the plants as it will help it as it grows. If you don't give your plant any support, then the plant is likely to topple over.

HOW TO LOOK AFTER YOUR BROAD BEANS AS THEY GROW

Broad beans don't take much looking after as they grow, but you there are a few things that you must make sure you do, from weeding, watering, feeding, staking and pinching out the tops.

Let me go over these in a little more detail:

Weeding

Your broad bean plants will grow much stronger and faster if the area around them is kept weed-free. Weeds tend to grow very fast, much faster than other plants, and therefore take away the light, water, and any goodness in the soil.

If you sow your broad bean seeding directly in the soil, then it is vital that you regularly weed the soil where they are growing. If you weed weekly, then weeds won't be able to take hold, and you should be able to just pull out the weeds without digging and disturbing the growing seedlings.

Watering

Broad bean seeds don't like to sit in really wet or waterlogged soil, so make sure you are growing them in free draining soil. If you have clay soil, then before you sow your broad beans, incorporate lots of well rotted manure, and some sharp sand into the soil. Fork this is very well, and this will help break up the clods of clay.

When you first plant your broad bean seeds, water the trough you sow them in, and then you shouldn't need to water again for a couple of weeks. As the weather gets hotter, and your plants grow larger, they will need watering more often. But don't water any more than twice a week, even in a very hot summer.

If you sow your broad bean seeds in October or November, water when you sow them, but then you most probably won't need to water again until the following spring. If, however, you live in a very dry or hot climate you will need to water your seeds at least once a week.

In the UK we have enough rain over the winter, so watering your broad beans isn't necessary.

Feeding

Broad beans are very hungry plants, and will benefit from regular feeding. You can use whatever feed you like, either general liquid plant feed that you mix with water, or pellets that you sprinkle on the soil and lightly fork in, or dust fertilisers that you scatter on the top of the soil. There are so many to choose from, and it depends on what you prefer, and how much you are willing to spend.

Go to your local garden centre to see the range they have, then you can make your choice.

The feed I prefer to use is **Shropshire Seaweed Fertiliser**, and this is only available to buy online.

Whatever feed you choose, follow the instructions on the bottle or packet.

Only start feeding your plants when the flowers start to form, and no earlier. If you feed your plants too early, it will encourage the plant to keep producing leaves and not many flowers. From the flowers come the bean pods, so you want to encourage the plant to produce more flowers and not leaves.

Staking

Some broad beans don't need staking, because if you have planted several rows of broad beans, they tend to support each other as they grow.

Also dwarf broad beans will only grow to about 18 inches, so are able to support themselves.

> If you do need to support your broad bean plants, it's very easy. All you need are some bamboo canes.

Make sure the bamboo cane is at least 4 foot long, broad bean plants can grow to 3 foot tall, and you'll need to make sure the support is pushed in the ground far enough.

Get your bamboo cane and place it about 2 inches away from the base of the broad bean plant. Push the cane into the soil as far as you can, at least 6 inches, but more if you're able.

Using garden string, carefully tie the broad bean plant to the cane every 9 inches. This will help secure the plant, and stop it getting top heavy and falling over and breaking. Tie it fairly loosely, as the plant will need some space to move.

Make sure you use garden string as it is soft, don't use metal ties, as these will rub against the stem of the plant and cut into it.

Pinching out the top

As your broad bean plant gets taller, and summer gets nearer, flowers on your broad beans will start to appear.

Broad bean flowers come in a variety of colours from white, pink, mauve through to a deep red. It depends what colour your seeds are to what colour your flowers are going to be.

The flowers grow from the main stem, only at the top half of the plant.

Because the flowers are bright, they will encourage all sorts of pollinators to come and harvest the nectar. This in turn helps the bean pods to grow.

As soon as the first beans start to grow from the flowers, pinch out the top 3 inches of each plant. You can either do this with your nails, or with a pair of secateurs. The top 3 inches of the plant produces leaves that are very tasty and will attract the black bean aphid.

Cutting off the tops of your broad bean plants helps stop the black bean aphids descending on you plants and ruining them, but also makes sure the plant puts all its energy into producing wonderful fat pods and beans.

PESTS AND DISEASES

Broad beans are fairly trouble-free when it comes to pests and diseases. Many problems can be sorted out very easily, but there are a few that you should watch out for.

Black bean aphids

These can appear overnight and can cover your plants very rapidly. If you get these, you won't get 1 or 2, but hundreds will cover your broad bean plants.

Even though they look awful, they can be sorted out, and got rid of very easily.

You can buy a general bug spray from your local garden centre, or for a fraction of the price, you can make your own ecological version.

To make your own bug spray, get a clean plastic spray bottle. These can usually be picked up very cheaply from your local DIY store or garden centre.

Squeeze in 1 teaspoon of washing up liquid, and then fill the rest of the bottle with cold water from the tap. You'll have to put the water in slowly, as lots of bubbles will be produced if you run the water too fast. Don't be tempted to use any more washing up liquid, because it could kill your plants.

At the first sign of the black bean aphid, spray the little bugs with the diluted washing up liquid mixture. Position the spray bottle about 9 inches away from the aphids, and give them a quick spray. Aphids breathe through their skin, so the soapy spray clogs up their skin, and therefore they can't breathe and suffocate. Once they are dead, if they don't get eaten by the ladybirds or other birds, they'll just slip off your plants. They are attracted to the tender shoots at the very top of the broad bean plant, so make sure that when the flowers start to appear, you snip off the top 3 inches of your broad bean plants.

If you leave your aphids untreated, they will destroy your plants and you won't be able to harvest any of your fresh beans.

Weevils

Pea and bean weevils are around in early spring, so keep an extra special eye on your plants as they are growing.

You'll know if you have weevils, because you will find small bite marks round the edges of the leaves of your broad bean plants.

If your plants are strong and sturdy, then they can cope with a few nibbled leaves, but very young plants may struggle, and your plants won't grow to their full potential. Try and cover small broad bean plants with a fleece to help protect them.

There are sprays you can buy if you notice any nibbled leaves, but if you weed and hoe around the base of the plants regularly, then you should be able to prevent this problem for occurring.

If your broad bean plants are effected by weevils, it will only be in spring.

Chocolate spot

This is a rare disease, but one that needs to be dealt with very promptly.

If you notice small, dark brown spots your broad bean leaves, then you will have chocolate spot.

If left untreated, this can wipe out your entire crop. As soon as you notice any effected plants, dig them up immediately and throw them away. Do not, under any circumstances put them in the compost heap as this will spread the disease.

Chocolate spot is a fungal disease, and thrives in cool, damp conditions, so is more prevalent between early winter to early spring.

There is no spray for infected plants, but the best way to avoid this disease is to make sure you don't grow your broad beans too close together. Air circulation is very important at keeping pests and diseases at bay.

> Also buy new seeds every year from a reputable seed company. These seeds would have been growing under controlled conditions and are disease free.

Rust

If you notice on your broad bean plants, leaves and stems, small brown dots surrounded by a yellow circle, then your plants have rust.

> Rust is a fungus disease, but is not as much of a threat to your

plant as chocolate spot. However a severe attack can cause all the leaves of your plant to fall off.

If you only have a little rust of a few plants, then this won't effect your crop. However if your plants have a severe attack of rust, then you need to pull up the infected plants and throw them in the bin. Do not put infected plants on the compost heap, as the spores can survive over winter and then the following year they will spawn again.

To prevent rust from forming, make sure that you don't grow your plants too close together, so the air can circulate round the plants. There are no sprays available that will get rid of rust on your broad bean plants.

WHEN TO HARVEST YOUR BROAD BEANS

Broad beans are best harvested when the beans are smaller inside. That way the skins of the beans haven't started to form and the bean is sweet and soft, rather than hard and bitter.

If you have sown your broad bean seeds in October, then you can start to harvest your beans as early as May, but if you've not sown your broad bean seeds until March, then they will be ready to harvest in August.

The best way to check to see if your broad beans are ready, is to harvest one pod from down the bottom of the plant, open the pod, and see what size the beans are. If the beans are about the size of your thumbnail, or a little smaller, then they are ready.

How to harvest your broad beans

Where the pods joins the stem of your broad bean plant, it is very thick, so pulling off the pods, can be quite difficult. Also, you may break the stem of the main plant, and therefore the plant won't grow anymore.

So the best way to get your pods off, is to use a pair of secateurs.

Start from the lowest pod on the plant and work your way up.

You don't have to harvest all your pods all together, but if you leave the pods on the plant for too long, then the beans will get tougher and taste less sweet.

How to store broad beans

When you have harvested your broad bean pods, if you are not going to use any that night for dinner, you can store the podded beans in the fridge, but only for a couple of days. Store them in a paper bag, or just on the fridge shelf. Don't store them in a plastic bag as they will sweat and go mouldy.

If you have not eaten your broad beans after a couple of days, they must be podded and then frozen.

If you have removed your broad beans from their pods, they must be used that same day. The broad beans will not keep very well once they are out of their pods.

Freezing your broad beans

Broad beans freeze very well, and they don't go mushy when defrosted.

You do need to blanche your broad beans before you freeze them. Blanching is a very important process, it cleans the surface of the broad beans of dirt and bugs, and helps your broad beans retain their bright green colour, as well as stopping them from loosing lots of their vitamins and minerals.

When you want to use your broad beans, just take out what you need, and leave what you don't need in the freezer for another time.

Blanching

Blanching is very easy to do and doesn't take very long.

- Half fill a large saucepan with water and bring to the boil. When the water is boiling, empty the broad beans into the water. Bring the water back up to the boil, and boil for 1 minute.
- In the meantime, get a large bowl and half fill it with very cold water.
- When the broad beans have boiled for 1 minute, take them out, and immediately put them in the cold water.
- The cold water will set the green colour of the beans, and also stop the cooking.
- Leave the beans in the cold water for 2 minutes and then drain well and put in a sealed plastic bag and in the freezer.

RECIPE - BROAD BEAN SPRING SALAD

Ingredients

For the salad:

- A couple of big handfuls of fresh or frozen broad beans (defrosted)
- 200g of Feta cheese, roughly crumbled
- 50g of whole pecans, roughly chopped
- 80g prosciutto

For the vinaigrette

- Juice of 1 lemon
- Juice of half a lime
- 125ml of olive oil
- Salt and pepper

Method

1. Pre heat the oven to Gas 6, 200C, or 400F.
2. Lay the prosciutto in a single layer, on a baking tray, and roast in the oven for 5 minutes.
3. Fill a saucepan with water and bring to the boil.
4. When the water boils, put in the broad beans, and boil for 3-5 minutes. When they are tender, they are cooked. Drain and put in a clean glass bowl.
5. Make the vinaigrette, by combining all the ingredients together, and whisking thoroughly.
6. Pour the vinaigrette on top of the broad beans and give them a toss. Because the beans are still warm, they will absorb the vinaigrette really well.
7. When the prosciutto is cooked, it will be crispy. Allow it to cool slightly, then break each slice into 4 or 5 pieces. Place in the bowl on top of the broad beans.
8. Drain the feta and crumble in with the broad beans.
9. Roughly chop the pecans and add those in with the broad beans as well.
10. Carefully mix together and then place on a serving plate.

CARROTS

INTRODUCTION

Carrots are a very versatile root vegetable. They can be boiled, roasted, sautéed and even mashed. They can be eaten raw, whole, cut into pieces, or even grated into salad or coleslaw.

They are not only a wonderful vegetable to accompany any meal, but they also are amazing inside a beautifully moist carrot cake, with the added bonus of some cream cheese icing on top.

I like to roast my carrots on their own, or with other vegetables underneath a whole chicken. Once the chicken is cooked, remove the chicken and let it rest under some foil, and then roast the vegetables a little longer so the edges get slightly charred and crispy.

Carrots are naturally sweet, which makes them able to be used in both sweet and savoury dishes. They come in many different colours and shapes, some you may have heard of, but others may be new to you.

Carrots are **root vegetables**, which means they grow under the soil and part of the plant's root becomes fleshy and enlarged.

The carrots that we use today have come from wild carrots. These were whitish in colour. They date back to Roman times, but these may have been what we call parsnips and not carrots at all. So there is a little bit of confusion as to when they were first discovered.

You can grow white carrots today (I have grown some myself), they're called Lunar White, and the seeds can be bought from **Pennard Plants.**

We have to go to 10th century Persia to confirm the first findings of the carrots that we all know and love today. Although they weren't orange, but purple or white and very thin. Then a mutation occurred and the purple colouring went, and yellow carrots came about and then our orange carrots evolved from those.

It seems that carrots were first cultivated from the wild carrots in Afghanistan and the surrounding areas in the 10th century. Before then, carrots grew wild in my countries with a temperate climate.

You hear of wild animals being domesticated over time, but in the case of carrots these have also, over time, been domesticated. Sounds odd, but it's true. Over the centuries carrots have become sweeter, brighter, less bitter, and more resilient to diseases.

Carrots come in a variety of colours: purple, yellow, white, red, black, and orange. Whatever their colour, they are grown in exactly the same way. Many are sown in March, but others in April.

Carrots are rich in beta carotene, which the body converts into vitamin A. They also have potassium, vitamin K, vitamin B6, and biotin in them. So they are very useful for your body.

When I was little I was always told that carrots help you see in the dark, so I always thought it made your eyes glow like torches, but now I know it's all to do with the vitamin B6 that helps your eyes stay healthy.

VARIETIES OF CARROTS

Carrots come in all different shapes, sizes, and colours these days, so it's your own personal preference as to which ones you would like to grow.

Over the years I've tried many different varieties from various different seed companies and some have worked better than others. Here are a few suggestions on my favourites.

If you are growing your carrots in a **container** that doesn't have much depth, then you need to grow shorter carrots.

The ones I would recommend are:

- Paris Market Atlas from Victoriana Nursery
- Little Finger from Pennard Plants
- Royal Chantenay 3 from Mr Fothergill's Seeds

All these varieties are short and stumpy, so are perfect for growing in small containers. They are also very good for children to grow, because when you harvest them, they are the right size to just eat straight away.

If you're growing in the **open soil**, then I would suggest the following varieties:

- **Autumn King 2 from Mr Fothergill's Seeds.** These are large and orange.
- **Cosmic Colour Collection from Victoriana Nursery.** These come in a variety of colours from white, yellow, red, orange and purple.
- **Lunar White from Pennard Plants.** I mentioned these earlier and they taste beautiful and are an interesting addition to the dinner plate.
- **Night Bird from Suttons.** These are long black carrots.

Of course there are many more varieties, so the choice is yours as to which ones you would like to grow and eat. Try a couple of varieties this year, and then another couple next year. You'll soon decide which ones you prefer and which ones suit your growing conditions.

PREPARING THE SOIL

Carrots grow best in light, sandy, fine soil. But if you have heavy clay or chalky soil then stick with only growing thick, sturdy carrots like **Autumn King, Eskimo F1**, or **Chanteney Red Cored 2.**

Preparing the open soil

When preparing the open soil, make sure that you have thoroughly weeded the area of soil where you are going to grow your carrot seeds. Also remove as many stones as you can.

Have you ever seen a three legged carrot or other bizarre shaped carrot? I'm sure you have, and I've harvested a few in my time.

The reason this happens is because as the carrot is growing, it suddenly comes into contact with a stone. The growing carrots can't

move the stone out the way, or grow through it, so it has to grow around it. So the best way to avoid any strange shaped carrots is to try and remove as many stones as you can.

Once you have weeded and removed the stones, also make sure that there aren't any large lumps of soil, if there are, break them down. Then level off the soil to make it even.

It is best to grow carrots in soil that doesn't have any horse manure in, because sometimes there are large lumps of, well, poo in it. This will also make your carrots grow into bizarre shapes. If you have manure that is very fine, then it can be added to the soil, but make sure you mix it in very thoroughly.

Preparing a container

If you are growing your carrots in a container, make sure that there are drainage holes in the bottom on the container so the excess water can drain away.

Put a few large stones at the very bottom of the container, as this will also help with drainage and stop the holes clogging up.

Then fill the container, nearly to top, with a mixture of multipurpose compost and sand. The contents will settle and go down a little.

WHEN AND HOW TO SOW YOUR CARROTS

When to sow your carrot seeds

Not all carrots are sown at the same time, so check your packets of seeds for the times they recommend, but generally most carrot seeds get sown in March or April time.

Carrots will not germinate if it is too cold, so if the weather is still a little on the chilly side then hold off from sowing your carrot seeds until the weather has warmed up a bit.

If you are able to protect your growing seeds with a cloche, then you can sow them a little earlier.

Don't sow all your carrot seeds together because they will all be ready to harvest together, and you can't eat 300 carrots in one go!

The best thing to do is to sow your carrots **successionally**. Sowing **successionally** basically means that you sow one row in the middle of March, then another row in the middle of April, then another row in the middle of May, and so on. This will give you a good supply of carrots throughout the season.

Carrots can be sown until July, but be aware that if you do sow some in June or July they will need much more watering as the seeds develop, this is because of the heat in summer.

How to sow your carrot seeds

Whether you are growing your carrot seeds in the open soil or in a container they need to be sown in exactly the same way:

- Using a long piece of string, mark out a row, making it as long you want to.
- If you want to sow two or more rows of carrots, make sure the rows are at least six inches apart from each other.
- Using a trowel, make a shallow trough about 1 inch deep all the way along the string. The best way to do this is to turn your trowel on its side and using the scoop of the trowel to carefully move the soil.

When you've made your trough, water the trough thoroughly.

I do this for several reasons: firstly it levels out the soil, it also helps your carrot seeds stick to the soil when you sow then, and don't get blown away on the breeze, and finally the seeds are then immediately in contact with some water so they can start to grow.

Once the water has drained down through the trough, it's time to sow your carrot seeds.

Place some seeds in the palm of one hand and then, using your thumb and finger from your other hand, pinch up some seeds.

Moving your finger and thumb back and forth, sprinkle the carrot seeds fairly thinly in the damp trough.

You don't have to be exact with your sowing, but try and make sure the seeds are about 5mm apart from each other. I'm not asking you to get down on your hands and knees with a tape measure to see how far apart each seed is from each other, that is unless you really want to.

Sprinkle the seeds in the trough until you get to the end of your row. Then very carefully move the soil back over the seeds and gently pat down the soil.

Put a label at one end of the line and a stick at the other end of the line, then you'll know where the line begins and ends.

If you are sowing your seeds in March and April you won't need to water them for a few days, but if you're sowing some carrot seeds in June or July you will most probably have to give them a careful water every day so they don't dry out.

WHAT THE FIRST LEAVES LOOK LIKE

After a couple of weeks you should start to see tiny little carrot shoots appear above the soil. They'll look like two long, thin green leaves. These are the baby leaves. As soon as these little leaves appear, protect them immediately from slugs and snails. I never used to have any problems with these slippery little gastropods eating my carrot leaves, but the last couple of years they have nibbled any that I've not protected.

The simplest way to protect them is to sprinkle a few pellets along the line, but crushed egg shells, dog hair, sawdust, old coffee grounds, or sand will do the trick just as well.

Water the new emerging seedlings very carefully as you don't want to disturb them as they grow, because when they first emerge, they are very small and delicate. As your seedlings grow larger, more leaves will appear, and the rest of the leaves will look like the carrot leaves that we know and love. Once your leaves look quite substantial, then there is no need to protect them from slugs and snails anymore.

THINNING OUT YOUR CARROTS

Now this you don't have to do, it just depends how thinly you sowed your carrot seeds first of all, and also how many of you seeds have germinated.

Carrots need space to grow and swell out, so if you have some carrots growing that are very close together then you may want to pull just a few out of the soil to give the rest of them a little bit more room.

If you do need to remove any carrot seedlings from the soil, make sure you do it very carefully and don't disturb any of the other carrots growing around them.

If you disturb any of the soil around the carrots, then make sure that you pat any soil that you've disturbed back down immediately. The reason for this is because the smell of the carrots will be released into the air and it will attract **carrot fly**. I will talk more on **carrot fly** in the **pests and diseases** chapter.

Once you have thinned out your carrot seedlings give the remaining carrots a good water to help settle the soil back down again.

HOW TO LOOK AFTER YOUR CARROTS AS THEY GROW

Carrots are fairly easy to look after, they're not fussy.

Water them about once a week, unless you have regular rain. When the seedlings are small make sure you water with a fine spray on your hose, or use a rose on a watering can.

However, when the carrots are well established then you don't have to be as careful with your watering. You can just use either a hose or a watering can without any end attachments. This way the water will go straight down into the soil and down to the roots of the carrots encouraging them to grow longer.

If you have a drought then you may need to water your carrots twice a week. The **tap root** of the carrots, which is the root at the very bottom, instinctively grows down into the soil to find water.

If you don't water regularly your carrots won't reach their full potential. If you have a sudden heavy downpour, you may find that your carrots split down the side. If they do split or grow into funny shapes, don't worry about it because your carrots will still taste amazing.

Also, make sure that you keep the area round your carrots free from weeds. If you don't, then the weeds will grow much faster than your carrots, and will eventually cover your growing carrot seedlings and then your carrots will die. The weeds will also take any goodness from the soil.

When you water your carrots, add some **Shropshire Seaweed Fertiliser** to the water. This will give your growing carrots lots of goodness, and help them grow big and strong.

PESTS AND DISEASES

There are only a few pests and diseases that your carrots can get. Some I have never had, but others are quite a big problem. I will mention the ones that I have had to cope with before.

Carrot fly

This can be major problem when growing carrots. I'm sure most of us have all suffered from this horrible little pest at least once. The smell of the carrots attracts the flies, which lay their eggs in the growing carrots, and then the eggs hatch and the little maggots nibble their way through the carrots.

You know when your carrots have fallen victim to the dreaded carrot fly because you will see black lines round the outside of you carrots when you harvest them.

There is no treatment for this, but it can be prevented, and here are a few suggestions on how this can be done:

Firstly, carrot fly can only fly up to about 18 inches off the ground, so if you make a barrier about 24 inches high out of plastic, or net curtains (make sure there are no holes in it) around your carrot bed, then this should prevent the carrot flies getting in.

If you are growing your carrots in a raised bed that is high enough you shouldn't have to worry about making a barrier. I knew someone who used to grow his carrots in a bath tub, an old one of course, not one that he used. This was the perfect height to stop the carrot fly getting to his crop. With an old bath tub you don't need to worry about drainage holes, as long as you don't block up the plug hole, you'll be fine.

Another way to stop carrot fly in their tracks is to grow alternate rows of carrots and onions next to each other. The smell from the onions drives away the carrot fly. If you don't have onions, then garlic, spring onions, or leeks will work just as well.

Also make sure that when you thin out your carrot seedlings, that you disturb the soil as little as possible, and cover up any carrots that are left in the soil really well.

Green top

This is exactly what it says it is. You may find that the tops of your carrots may turn a little green. This is nothing to worry about, you can still eat them and they are not poisonous. The sunlight has caused this and is easily sorted. The way to stop this is by covering the green part of the carrots with soil.

Split carrots

This is caused when your carrots have suddenly been given a huge amount of water. Usually this happens after a heavy down pour, or if you don't water them regularly enough. Make sure you water your carrots at least once a week, but twice a week during a drought.

A heavy downpour is something we can't control, so if you are due a huge amount of rain, maybe don't water your carrots the day before.

Forked carrots

This is where your carrot has been growing quite happily and then they hit something hard and the root separates and you end up with a two-, three- or even more-legged carrot.

To stop this from happening make sure that before you sow your carrot seeds, you dig the soil very thoroughly and remove any stones or large pieces of soil. If you have heavy clay soil, try adding some sand to the soil to break down the large clumps.

Weird shaped carrots are very funny, and to be honest I don't mind finding the odd few. They taste just as good, and unless you're showing them it doesn't really matter what shape they are.

WHEN AND HOW TO HARVEST YOUR CARROTS

When to harvest

The time to harvest your carrots, depends on when you sowed them. If you sowed your carrot seeds in March, then they'll be ready to harvest in approximately June time.

Carrots are ready to harvest at any time, it's not like you have to wait for them to ripen. But carrots are usually harvested anytime between June until October.

It also depends what size you want your carrots to grow to. If you want larger carrots, then you can leave them in the ground for a little longer, but if you only want small, baby carrots, then you can harvest them earlier.

Before you start digging, the best way to check what size your carrots are is easy:

- Using your fingers, all you have to do is move a little of the soil from around the very top of a carrot away.
- If the top of the carrot is about 1 inch across, or more, then you should have a good sized carrot growing below the soil.
- If the top of your carrot is smaller than 1 inch, then replace the soil and leave it for another couple of weeks.

How to harvest

When harvesting your carrots use a large garden fork.

You will need to place the prongs on the fork about 3 inches away from the carrots. This will make sure that you don't pierce any of the carrots as you dig them up.

Push the fork prongs into the soil as far down as you can. Keep one hand on the handle of the fork and very carefully pull the fork back. With your other hand carefully hold the tops of the carrots and slowly pull the carrots out of the ground.

If you harvest your carrots this way it's much easier and you are less likely to snap any carrots.

As your carrots come out of the soil they will look wonderful. Shake the excess dirt off and hopefully you'll have some wonderfully straight carrots, but also the odd strange shaped one or two.

If you are harvesting your carrots from a container, do it the same way, but use a small trowel instead.

HOW TO STORE YOUR CARROTS

I don't usually need to store my carrots as I tend to harvest and eat them straight away.

But if you are going to store your carrots, you must make sure that you only store perfect carrots.

If they have any blemishes, splits or any abnormalities on them, you can't store them and they must be eaten as soon as possible.

If you store any carrots that aren't perfect, then they will go mouldy, and they will ruin the rest of your harvest.

If you are storing your carrots, you must make sure that you check them occasionally and if any are showing signs of problems, then you must remove them. If they are ok to eat then use them immediately, or if they are not suitable for eating then throw them away.

Before storing you carrots you must cut off most of the green leaves. Only leave about 1 inch above the top of the carrot.

Then get a sturdy wooden crate and put a good layer of sand in the bottom. Pat the sand down and then lay some carrots on the sand. Make sure none of the carrots touch each other. Then cover with more sand and repeat the process until the crate is full.

Store your crate in a cool shed or garage.

CARROT RECIPE

Usually when people cook carrots they tend to slice them and then boil them in water.

This is fine, but I've always thought there must be a more exciting way to cook carrots.

Carrots are naturally sweet, and so the best way to bring out their sweetness is to roast them. Let me show you how I roast mine.

Roasted carrots with chives

Ingredients:

- A selection of carrots, whatever colours you want
- Olive oil
- Salt and pepper
- Chives, finely chopped

Method:

1. Set your oven to Gas 5, 190 C, or 375 F.
2. Wash your carrots, but don't peel, unless you need to.
3. Cut your carrots in 1 inch chunks. Carrots will shrink a little while they roast, so make sure you don't cut them too small.
4. Put the chopped carrots on a baking tray and drizzle over a little olive oil and sprinkle on some salt and pepper and mix throughly.
5. Place on the middle shelf in your oven for about 20-25 minutes, turning once half way through the cooking.
6. When they are cooked sprinkle over the finely chopped chives and serve immediately.

CONTAINER GARDENING AND RAISED BEDS

INTRODUCTION

Growing your own fruits and vegetables at home doesn't need to take up lots of space.

Many people may want to grow only a few plants, but just don't have much spare time due to work. Maybe there are no allotments near to where you live, or maybe your garden is very small that you are unable to turn it in to a vegetable patch? Some people live in flats with a communal garden, or sometimes no garden at all.

Lots of people only want to grow one or two plants each year, just to be able to taste something so fresh and tasty.

Whatever your situation you can always grow something.

Be it some herbs on a sunny window sill, a few small pots out on your balcony, a small raised bed on your patio, or a few long raised beds at the end of a small garden.

In this book I will run through what containers you can use, what growing material to fill your containers with, where to buy raised beds, if you want to use them, and the plants that you can grow.

Remember, if you are worried about sowing plants from seed, or only want a couple of a certain type of plant, then you can always visit your local garden centre to see what they have on offer.

There is no shame is buying small plants and then looking after them as they grow.

WHAT CONTAINERS TO USE

You can use any type of container you like, be it plastic, wooden, terracotta, or some old wellington boots. But there are a few things that you must make sure your container has.

Firstly, your container must have holes in the bottom. Even if you have a small pot that is going to sit on your window sill, or a large wooden barrel that you are placing on your patio, it must have drainage holes in the bottom. If you don't put drainage holes in the base of your container then it will get water logged and the water will go stagnant and smell. The plants could possibly die as well.

Most plants don't like to sit in damp soil for too long, this can either stunt their growth, or worst of all, kill the plant.

Depending on how large your container is, make sure you have adequate drainage holes. Drainage holes should be about 2 inches apart from each other. If you have a container that you will be able to drill through, for example plastic or wood, then using the largest drill bit you have, make as many holes as you can, spacing them approximately 2 inches apart.

If you have a container made of terracotta, make sure you only buy the containers that have drainage holes already in the bottom of the pot. It is very difficult to make drainage holes in these pots, and you are very likely to break the pot if you try to make some yourself.

Secondly, make sure the container is the right size for the plants you are planning on growing. For example, don't plant a pumpkin plant in a small container. The pumpkin roots will need room to grow and spread out.

Think about how tall and wide your plant will grow and this will give you a rough idea how much root space it is going to need. A rough guide for this is to look how wide the plant will grow. The roots usually spread as wide as the plant. It is always best to give a plant more room than it needs.

You can always create a herb bed in a large container. But be aware if you are growing any variety of mint, as this will spread and take over the container. Mint will smother any other plants growing and kill them, so always make sure you grow any varieties of mint in a container on their own.

And finally, look at what space you have where you live to put any containers. You may only have a few sunny window sills, or if you have a very small back garden. You many only want a few containers or raised beds in one area.

It's always best to start with a few containers and then you can always add more. Having a container garden does look wonderful, and it's surprising what you are able to achieve with just a few simple pots of various sizes.

RAISED BEDS - WHAT TO MAKE THEM OUT OF

Raised beds are a wonderful invention. Yes they can cost quite a bit of money, but once you have them, they will last for about 15 years, maybe longer.

Raised beds can be made whatever size you need them, but make sure that your raised beds are at least 18 inches high. This will then be deep enough for your potatoes to grow, as well as give enough stability for your bamboo canes if you are growing climbing beans.

It is also preferable to make sure that your raised beds are no wider than 4 foot, because otherwise you won't be able to reach the middle. But your raised beds can be as long as you need them to be.

There are several ways to make your raised beds, you can go and buy some timber from your local DIY store. Make sure that you buy timber that has been treated and kiln dried. Timber that has been treated won't rot as quickly and will therefore last much longer.

You need solid timbers, and wooden fence posts are a very good choice. The fence posts come in various lengths, but make sure you get fence posts where the width and depth are the same. These will sit together better and you'll get a more even finish to your raised bed.

Some people use gravel boards, but these are fairly thin. Just think about how much soil is going to be in your raised bed and the weight of that pushing against the wood. Gravel boards will soon break. You can also use railway sleepers, but these are very expensive.

You will also need to buy some wooden stakes as well. These will need to be placed in each corner and at least every metre to hold the raised bed in place. You'll also need to buy some very long galvanised nails or screws, because you'll need to nail the raised bed timbers to the stake.

Making your own raised beds from scratch is very time consuming and usually takes at least two people to put them together.

Raised beds can also be made out of paving slabs, or you can build them out of bricks, but again this is rather difficult. If you are creating raised beds out of these materials, you'll also have to use concrete to fix them together. Once they are in place they are very sturdy and, unlike timber raised beds, they will not rot. Over the course of many years you will find that some of the bricks or paving slabs may come loose, but these are easily repaired.

Concreting is not an easy task, and unless you are a builder this isn't something that most people can do. So you may have to call in a professional which may cost you quite a bit of money.

Brick raised beds don't blend in with the garden as good as timber raised beds do. Over the course of several years they will get more weathered and moss will start to grow on them, but this does take quite while.

If making your own raised beds from scratch sounds too stressful, and buying and cutting everything to the correct size is too daunting. Then finding out you've forgotten something, or miscalculated, and you have to go back to the store and, oh..... You end up getting very cross.

Then I would suggest investing in some raised beds from Woodblocx.

Woodblocx specialise in wooden raised beds, and they can be made to measure.

I have one small raised bed from Woodblocx at home, and it's a joy. Very soon I will be getting many more. All the wood came pre-sawn, and everything that I needed to make my raised bed was there. There are no nails or cement.

All I had to do was remove the contents from the box, read their very simple instructions and then in under an hour, I had put my new raised bed together.

All you'll need to put your raised beds together is a hammer and a lovely cup of tea and possibly a couple of biscuits.

Then all I had to do was to filled my raised bed with a mixture of soil and manure and then start planting.

Check them out, they're amazing. I'd go for them every time: https://www.woodblocx.co.uk/

WHAT TO FILL YOUR RAISED BEDS OR CONTAINERS WITH

Containers

Whatever size your container is, and whatever it is made of, before you put anything in your container, you must first make sure that there are enough drainage holes in the bottom of your container. Containers can be made of anything, it could be half a wooden barrel, a terracotta pot, and old sink or bath, even an old pair of wellington boots.

Whatever you choose, you must make sure there are enough drainage holes in the bottom, otherwise the water will be unable to drain through and the standing water in the container will go stagnant and smell.

Once the drainage holes are made, get some large stones, or broken terracotta pots (these are sometimes referred to as crocks) and place a thin layer in the bottom of your container. These will stop the holes getting clogged up with soil, and will allow the water to drain through easily. These crocks will also give a bit of weight to any light containers, and stop it from being blown over in a strong wind.

Then you need to fill your container with a mixture of multi purpose compost and well rotted manure. Mix these together and then fill your contain to the very top. The manure will also help the water drain through as well as giving your plants a good feed. Do three parts compost to one part manure. This will give you a lovely mix for your plants to grow it.

Once you have filled your container, give the contents a level off and then a gentle pat down. The contents will settle a little more over the next few days. If you want to encourage the contents of your container to settle a little quicker, then water thoroughly using a rose on the end of your watering can spout.

Raised beds

With raised beds you don't have to worry about drainage holes, because raised beds don't have a bottom! Raised beds are just sides.

Raised beds usually have to be built in situ. Which means you need to build it where you want it to be. Raised beds are heavy, and are very difficult to move, so make sure that you choose the right place for your raised beds before you start making it.

Once you have built your raised beds then they need to be filled as follows:

Firstly lay some flattened cardboard boxes in the base of your raised bed. Makes sure that they are thick boxes, and you can over lap the boxes if necessary. Placing cardboard boxes in the bottom of your raised bed stops any weeds or grass growing.

Doing this will stop most weeds, but if you place a raised bed where wild brambles grow, you will need to make sure you removed any brambles before hand. Wild brambles will grow through anything.

The cardboard will biodegrade but, by the time it has, the grass and weeds underneath would have died.

On top of your cardboard you will then need to put a lovely thick layer of wood chips. About 2 inches would be ideal. If you know a tree surgeon, hopefully you can get some for free. The wood chips will hold down the cardboard, help with drainage, and will eventually rot down.

Then to fill the remainder of your raised bed you will need some soil. Check the soil before you buy it, as some soil you buy is really awful and full of all sorts of rubbish. You need soil that is fairly fine in texture, but when you squeeze a handful of it together it stays in a clump, but once your touch it again it falls apart. Also make sure that it doesn't have too many stones in it. Mix into the soil some well rotted manured and a small amount of ballast, which is a mixture of sand and small stone. This will also help with the drainage.

Make sure that your ballast only consists of sand and stones and doesn't have any cement in it.

Again mix three parts soil to 1 part manure. Don't add too much ballast, it all depends on the size of your bed as to how much you will need to add. Mix the ballast in last and give it a mix around. Remember you can always add a little more ballast in, but it's very difficult to take out.

Look in your local DIY store for ballast:

What ever you choose, check before you buy. What you want is a majority of sand and lots of small smooth stones.

Fill your raised beds to the very top, smooth over with a rake and leave to settle for at least a week before planting anything. The contents of the raised bed will go down a little, which is what you would expect.

It will cost you quite a bit of money to fill your raised beds to start with, but once they're filled then that's it. In a couple of years time you may need to add a little more multi purpose compost and manure to them, just to top your raised beds up. If you have compost bins, and make your own compost, then you can use that.

WHAT TO PLANT IN YOUR CONTAINERS OR RAISED BEDS

You can really grow most plants in containers or raised beds. But you must make sure that if you are growing a large plant, that you grow it in a large pot or container.

The roots of your plants will need to spread, so make sure you give them sufficient room to do so.

If your plant isn't given enough room for it's roots to spread, then your plant won't reach its full potential and will be much smaller than you would have expected, also the plant will suffer and become stressed and could die.

Trees

Trees can be grown in containers and raised beds, but make sure that you choose the small dwarf trees either M9 (final tree height 7-8 foot) or M27 (final tree height 5 foot). If you are growing a fruit tree in a container or raised bed, make sure that whatever container or raised bed you use is at least 2 foot deep and 3 foot wide. This will allow the trees roots to spread, but you must also water frequently, at least once a week until your tree is established, and then every couple of weeks during its growing season. Make sure you water very well.

Trees are thirsty plants and they would also benefit from some Shropshire seaweed fertiliser once the blossoms and fruit are growing.

Strawberries

Strawberries will grow very well in containers. You can buy a strawberry barrels for growing your strawberries in. Strawberry barrels are very useful if you are limited on room in your garden, and they are very easy to plant your strawberries in.

Do remember that when the barrel is full, it will be very heavy and you won't be able to move it. So before you start to fill your barrel, get it in place.

Use a mixture of well rotted horse manure and multi purpose compost and put some in the base. Fill until you get to the lowest holes. Then, working from the outside of the barrel, carefully place one strawberry plant in each hole, making sure the roots are on the inside of the barrel, and the green leaves are on the outside. Water the plants in well, and then fill the barrel with more compost and manure until you reach the next set of holes and repeat as before. Continue until you reach the top. Once the barrel is full you can plant some more strawberry plants at the very top.

When watering the plants make sure that you water each plant separately. Don't water from the top because the plants at the bottom won't get any water and they will die.

As the strawberries grow they will fill up the holes and then send out runners. Runners are the strawberries' way of producing more plants, At the beginning of the season cut these runners off because the plant will stop producing fruit. Once you have harvested all your fruits then let the runners grow and keep these new plants if you wish. Strawberry plants will last about 3 or 4 years, so if you start to save some of the runners from the second year, you can replace any plants that are past their best.

Make sure you feed your strawberry plants at least once a week once the flowers appear, and keep feeding until they have stopped fruiting.

Potatoes

Potatoes can be grown in special grow bags that can be bought from either Mr Fothergill's Seeds, Thompson and Morgan, or most well known seed companies. You can either buy the cheap bags that will only last one year, or spend a little more money to buy the reusable ones. Potatoes will also grow very well in large plastic pots. The best pots to buy are from Stewart Garden and they come in three colours, black, green and brown. They can be found in most garden centres or online in the UK. If you have a 12 inch pot then they will be perfect for planting just one seed potato in, but you can also get 15 inch pots, and these are big enough to plant two seed potatoes in.

In the base of your pot sprinkle a mixture of well rotted manure and multi purpose compost, this need to be about 3 inches deep. Then add a little potato feed, this is a slow release feed for your growing potatoes, and can usually be bought when you buy your seed potatoes from online seed companies. Place your seed potato on top of the mixture and then fill the rest of the pot with more manure and compost. Water well and place your pots in a sunny spot and water when the soil looks dry.

Herbs and Salad

Troughs are also brilliant for growing a selection of herbs or salad in. Depending on how much room your have, a small trough can fit on a window sill, and you can plant three or four different herb plants in one trough. I would suggest chives, parsley (curly or flat), basil and thyme. These herbs I use more frequently in my cooking.

If you are wanting to grow any variety of mint, then please make sure that you grow this in a pot all by itself. It will take over and smother any other plants in the same pot. Mint comes in many different varieties from spearmint, apple mint, pineapple mint, lemon balm, ginger mint as well as several others.

When planting in a container use all the available space in your pot. If you are growing a tall plant like a sprouting broccoli, these take a long time to grow, so use the space around the base of your broccoli and grow some lettuce, radish, a couple of bush tomatoes or some spring onions. Some plants that won't disturb the soil much when you harvest them.

You could grow your French beans up a wigwam, then around the base grow some dwarf kale or spinach.

You can grow whatever you like in containers or raised beds.

Please also don't feel that you have to grow all you plants from seed. If you only have a small amount of space and are therefore growing all you plants in containers, pop along to your local garden centre and choose some plants. Once you get home and you plant them, you're still growing them and looking after them.

So just have fun with your containers and raised beds, grow what you want to eat.

SUGGESTIONS ON WHAT TO GROW IN A RAISED BED

If you are limited on space, then making the most of your containers and raised beds is very important.

I am going to suggest ways of making the most out of a small raised bed, which measures one metre square.

If I put suggestions down for containers raised beds of various sizes then this book would never end. So if your container or raised bed is different then you'll just have adjust it a little, but hopefully this will give you some ideas of what you can grow in a fairly small space.

Put a layer of cardboard at the bottom of your raised bed, then a layer of wood chips, then fill your raised bed right to the very top, with a mixture of three parts soil, one part manure, and about three handfuls of ballast. Make sure you level the contents off and then give it a firm pat down.

You need to make the most of your one metre square space, so you'll need to be very organised.

Decide what you would like to eat. There is no point in growing fruits or vegetables that you don't like. You will also need to choose crops that grow fairly fast and don't need much room to grow.

In my one metre square raised bed I will be growing the following:

Mixed lettuce leaves, radishes, bush tomatoes, spring onions, climbing French beans, cucamelons, courgette, carrots, chives, parsley, spinach, dwarf kale, pak choi, choi sum, beetroot, sugar snap peas and corn salad.

Mark out nine equal squares, which in my bed will all be about one foot square. The easiest way to do this is to use sand and sprinkle it on top of the soil. It will look like a naughts and crosses board.

So that I don't forget what I want to grow in each square, I will then write on some plant labels what I will be planting. I will also make a plan on some paper as well.

Courgettes

In one square I will plant a courgette plant "One Ball" which is available from Victoriana Nursery Gardens. This is a compact plant, so won't trail all over the place. Make sure you plant this in one of the corner squares as it will spread a little bit.

Carrots

Then in another square I will grow some carrots. I want a variety of colours of carrots, but don't want to buy all sorts of packets, I will grow "Cosmic Colour" which are a wonderful array of colours from yellow through to purple. These can also be bought from Victoriana Nursery Gardens.

Cucamelons, spring onions and radish

For another square, so I can get a bit of height in the raised bed, in the centre of the square I will put up a wigwam using 6 bamboo canes, all 4 foot in length. Push the canes into the soil as far as they will, go and then gather the tops of the canes together and tie them securely. Up each cane I will grow two cucamelon plants, sometimes these are called mouse melons. These can be found very widely now in most seed catalogues, but I get mine from Sutton Seeds.

Then around the wigwam, on one side I will be growing spring onions, white Lisbon are always a safe bet from Mr Fothergill's Seeds and on the other side I will be growing some radish. The variety of radish I love growing are called Bright Lights. These are very colourful and are also available from Mr Fothergill's Seeds.

Herbs — chives and parsley

Herbs are very important to grow as well, and they are very easy to grow in a raised bed. They always bring an extra dimension to your food. Make sure that you choose some herbs that will fit in the space you have, and will not get too big. Don't choose any form of mint because it will spread rapidly and completely take over. Also I would suggest not planting rosemary or sage and this does get very large. So in my one foot square space, I am going to choose chives and parsley. I will plant chives on one half and then parsley on the other half.

Climbing French beans, kale and spinach

In the very centre square, again it's good have some height in your raised bed, so again I'm going to make a wigwam out of just 6 bamboo canes. But this time the canes need to be at least 8 foot long. Push the canes into the soil as far as you can, and then gather the tops of the canes and tie them together firmly. Up each cane I'm going to plant two climbing French bean plants, I like Cobra and these can be bought from Thompson and Morgan.

You don't want to waste the space around the climbing French beans, so to fill up the remaining space in the square I will be growing spinach and kale. The spinach variety is Samish F1 from Mr Fothergill's Seeds, which is small, and the kale, I would recommend dwarf green curled also from Mr Fothergill's. Both these will not grow very tall, but will cover the soil and fill up the area.

Pak choi and choi sum

It's always good to grow something a little different, so in another square, I will be growing a mixture of Pak choi, the variety is called Colour and Crunch as well as some choi sum. Both these can be bought from Mr Fothergill's Seeds. These are a great addition to a stir fry.

Tomatoes and salad leaves

Now I expect you're wondering if you can grow tomatoes in a raised bed of this size, well yes you can, but you must choose the right variety. Tall tomatoes will take up too much room, so the best ones the choose are the bush varieties. Bush tomato plants are compact and if you grow your tomatoes in a corner section of your raised bed, you should be able to fit in 3 plants.

Make sure you plant you tomatoes on the outside of the square, so then they can cascade down the outside of the raised bed.

Bush tomatoes don't need side shooting either, so that's an extra bonus. Choose three different varieties, so you get different flavours, and it's up to you, but try and get three different colours as well. I would suggest Tumbling Tom Yellow from Mr Fothergill's Seeds, Gartenperle from Victoriana Nursery Gardens, and Green Sausage which you can also get from Victoriana Nursery Gardens. Then in any remaining space around the tomatoes, plant some Mixed Lettuce Leaves. Make sure that you grow the *cut and come again* variety. With this variety you just harvest the leaves, as and when you need them, and then more leaves will continue to grow. The variety that I come back to year after year is from Mr Fothergill's seeds and it's just called Mixed Salad leaves.

We're nearly there, just two more squares to go.

Beetroot

In another square I will plant a mixture of beetroot. You can just sow one variety if you like, but why not go for something different from Pennard Plants, their mixed packet of Caboodles of Bountiful Beetroot give you a wonderful variety of different sizes, shapes and colours. If however you want to stick with something reliable, then Boltardy from Victoriana Nursery Gardens always grow really well and are very dark red. If you would rather grow a light pink beetroot, then Chioggia make a lovely alternative from Mr Fothergill's Seeds.

Sugar snap peas, lambs lettuce

And finally in the last square, again for a little bit of height, I would make a little wigwam of six bamboo canes. These canes only need to be 4 foot high. Push the canes into the soil as far as they'll go and then tie the canes securely at the top and then plant 3 sugar snap pea seeds round each cane. The variety I like to grow are from Mr Fothergill's seeds and are called Nairobi. These are a heavy cropper, and are crisp and taste fantastic. Then in the surrounding soil round the wigwam I would sow some more salad leaves, but this time something a little different, so you can get a contrast with the other salad leaves growing. So I would choose corn salad although it's also known as lamb's lettuce and can be found at most online seed companies, but I get mine from Victoriana Nursery Gardens. This again is a cut and come again plant, and will fill in the gaps around your growing sugar snap peas.

So that's my plan for my one metre square raised bed. It's surprising how much you can fit in to such a small space. You just need to be organised and plan what you are going to grow. Make a little design on a piece of paper, then it'll give you something to work towards.

You don't have to divide your bed into as many sections as I have, whatever is right for you. I've just given you some suggestions to help you. Because you are only growing a few of each plant, you most probably won't want to sow all your plants from seed. Pop along to your local garden centre and see what plants they have on offer. If you don't sow your plants from seed it doesn't matter, once you get all your plants home, you are then doing the hard work by helping them through the rest of their growing life.

Make sure that you water your raised bed frequently, small raised beds dry out quickly in the hot summer and during a heatwave they will need watering daily. Also make sure you feed with Shropshire seaweed fertiliser at least once a week.

If you have a good mixture of soil, manure and ballast in your raised bed, then this will help retain the moisture.

If all you have is a very small growing area, raised beds and container gardens are a perfect way for you to be able to grow just a few fruits and vegetables. You don't need a huge garden, or even an allotment to be able to grow your own, and I hope this book has given you a few suggestions on what you are able to grow even in a very small space.

COURGETTES

GROWING COURGETTES

Courgettes are very versatile and come in all sorts of different shapes and colours. In the UK we call them courgettes, but in other countries they are called zucchinis, some countries even refer to them as baby marrows. In this book, I will refer to them as courgettes.

Courgettes are from the Cucurbita family, which also includes pumpkins, squash, cucumbers, and some gourds.

Courgettes are a fruit because they have seeds inside them. They are not a vegetable. I know this seems really bizarre as we imagine a fruit as something you would keep in your fruit bowl with your apples. Maybe next time my son asks for an apple, I'll suggest he try a courgette instead? I can hear his reply now!

We all know that you eat the fruits of the plants (the courgettes), but you can also eat the flowers. They are beautiful when stuffed. Why not try mixing some pancetta, bacon or parma ham with cream cheese and adding in some fresh herbs?

Once the flowers are stuffed, make sure the tips of the flowers are closed, and then dip the flowers in batter, and deep fry until golden brown.

Courgettes originated in the 16th century and were grown in America. Back then courgettes were more like squashes with hard skins.

It wasn't until the 19th century, when they were grown more widely in Italy, that the courgettes developed softer skins. They became very popular, and these are the courgettes we eat today. Courgettes are widely grown across the Mediterranean.

We usually cook courgettes before we eat them, even though they are a fruit. But they can be eaten raw in salads.

Courgettes have a sweetness to them and are wonderful in both sweet and savoury dishes. They make an excellent addition to cakes and breads.

Courgettes can be cooked in many different ways. They are great roasted, fried in batter, stuffed, grilled, but my favourite way is to barbecue them.

Courgettes are very healthy, as they are low in fat and salt, as well as being very low in carbohydrates and sugars. They are an excellent source of protein, fibre, vitamin C and vitamin K, as well as many other minerals. Courgettes are very low in calories as they are mainly made up of water. This makes them an excellent vegetable if you are trying to lose weight. Obviously don't dip them in batter and deep fry them, as this adds on the calories.

DIFFERENT TYPES OF COURGETTES

Courgettes come in 3 different types: long green, long yellow or small round balls.

They all grow in the same way.

Let me go through these in a little more detail, and which varieties I would recommend.

Long green courgettes

These are the most popular courgettes to grow. If you want to grow some long green courgettes you'll need to harvest your courgettes when they are about 5 inches long. When you buy courgettes in the shops they tend to be much bigger than this. If you harvest your courgettes when they are smaller, they have a more delicate, sweet flavourer to them. If you allow your courgettes to get too large, they will start to taste bitter.

If a flower is still attached to the end of your courgette when you harvest it, it's not a problem. If you wish to harvest your courgettes when they are smaller than 5 inches you can. Courgettes are ready whatever size they are.

I would recommend you try "Defender F1" or "Endurance F1". Both will produce an excellent crop.

Long yellow courgettes

If you want to grow long courgettes, but don't want to grow green courgettes, I would suggest you try growing yellow courgettes. These grow in exactly the same way as green courgettes, but they have a wonderful dark yellow skin, and light yellow flesh.

Harvest these courgettes also when they reach about 5 inches long, but no longer. They will still be lovely and firm, and the seeds inside will still be small.

If you let your courgettes grow too large, the flesh will become watery and bitter. Not very nice.

There are only a few varieties of yellow courgettes to choose from. I would suggest you try either "Golden Dawn III F1" or "Orelia F1". These produce a really good harvest, and tasty fruits.

Small round ball courgettes

These are little balls of joy. If you don't want to grow long courgettes, then why not give the small round courgettes a go. They come in either dark green, light green or yellow, and you should be able to find at least a couple of varieties in your local garden centre. If you can't find any, you can always find a good selection online from the large seed companies.

Grow these as you would all your other courgettes. Usually you will harvest your fruits when they are between 2-6 inches across). If you let them grow too big, then the skins will get tough and the flesh will get watery and bitter.

The best way to cook round courgettes is to cut them in half and scoop out the seeds (there won't be many). Fill one half with a mixture of mince, peppers, onions, and cheese. Season with salt, pepper and herbs, and put the other half on the top. Roast in a medium oven for about 30-40 minutes. Making sure the meat is cooked through and the courgette is tender.

I would recommend you try growing a compact variety called "Eight Ball F1". The fruits are green and grow very well. If space is at a premium, then this variety will be perfect.

You could also try "One Ball". These are yellow and also a compact variety. The fruits are very meaty and have an excellent flavour and texture.

WHEN TO SOW YOUR COURGETTE SEEDS

Courgette seeds can be sown from March to the beginning of May in a greenhouse, cold frame or polytunnel. They can also be sown directly outside in the soil, but this must wait until May when the outside temperature is much warmer. Make sure you have sown your seed by the end of May otherwise the weather will get too hot for your seedlings and they may wilt and die.

Do not sow your courgette seeds any earlier than May, because the weather could still be too cold and damp, and your seeds will rot and not germinate.

The germination rate when sowing undercover or directly out in the soil is also quite different.

If you sow your courgette seeds undercover, the germination rate is much higher at about 90% germination. If you sow your courgette seeds directly in the soil outside the germination rate is much lower at about 50%.

Sowing courgette seeds undercover

I always sow my courgette seeds undercover in a greenhouse, but a polytunnel or cold frame will work just as well.

Always sow a couple of extra seeds than you need, just in case some don't germinate.

You can sow your courgette seeds undercover any time from March through to the beginning of May.

Courgette seeds are very easy to sow. This is how I sow mine:

- Fill a 3 inch pot to the top with multi purpose compost, I use J Arthur Bowers. Once the pot is full with compost, gently pat it down so that it is level.
- Once you have levelled off the compost you will want it to come nearly to the top of the pot. You may have to add a little more compost if it is too low.
- Courgette seeds are quite large, so you should only sow one seed per 3 inch pot. Always sow courgette seeds on their side, so the thin part of the seed is facing upwards. This way, the water won't sit on the seed and rot it. Also make sure that you can see both the pointed ends of the seed, and you haven't pushed one end right down into the soil.
- The reason for sowing your seeds this way is because the root bursts out of the seed first, and then the seed splits into 2 parts, so more of the plant can grow. If the seed is too far into the soil, the seedling will find it hard to push upwards towards the surface of the soil.
- Take one seed between your finger and thumb and push it 1-1.5 inches into the compost.
- Cover the seed with more compost and water each 3 inch

pot from above. Make sure you attach a rose onto the end of the watering can spout. Don't over water your seeds, as you don't want them to sit in wet soil for too long. If they do, the seeds will rot and not germinate.

- Allow the water to drain all the way through the compost.
- Water your seedlings every 3 or 4 days, but check that the compost is dry first. If the compost is still damp you will not need to water.
- Your courgette seeds should start to push through the compost in about 5-10 days.

Sowing courgette seeds directly in the soil

If you are sowing your courgette seeds directly outside in the soil, you must wait until May to sow them. Courgette plants are very delicate, especially when they are small, and if you have a late frost where you live, this will make the leaves wilt and die, and so will the plant.

Keep checking the weather in your area, and if a frost is not forecast 2 weeks before your last frost date then you can sow your seeds.

Before you sow your seeds in the soil, you must dig over the area you are going to use. Remove any weeds and any very large stones from near the surface. Roots from courgette plants spread out and down into the soil. But the roots will work their way round most obstacles.

Sprinkle onto the soil any organic matter, and then dig it into the soil. Courgettes are hungry plants, and love organic matter.

Once you have dug the soil over very well, cleared it of weeds, and large stones you will then need to rake it level.

Raking the soil will break down any clumps of soil that you may have missed and help get out any other unwanted obstacles for the soil.

Now you are ready to sow your courgette seeds.

Because the germination rate of courgette seeds is much lower when you sow them directly into the soil, you will need to sow a few seeds together. I would suggest sowing 2 or 3 seeds together. That way at least one seed will germinate from each group. If more that one seed germinates from the group, remove the weakest ones and only leave the strongest seedling to continue growing.

Using a trowel, dig a small hole in the soil, about 2 inches deep. Carefully put your courgette seeds in the hole, making sure you sow them on their sides. Then cover them with soil.

So you don't forget where you've sown your seeds, push a bamboo cane into the soil and insert a label.

Courgette plants need room to spread, so leave at least 2 feet - in each direction - between the next group of courgette seeds you sow.

Continue sowing your groups of courgette seeds until you have planted all you want.

Once you have sown your seeds, water the soil above the seeds. Make sure you use a rose on the end of your watering can spout. Water only when the soil is dry. To test to see if your soil is dry, push your finger into the soil. If the soil feels dry, then water, but if the soil feels wet you won't need to water.

Check the soil every 3-4 days and water if needed.

Your courgette seeds should start to pop through the soil in about 7-14 days. As soon as they do, you're going to have to protect them from slugs and snails.

PROTECTING FROM SLUGS AND SNAILS

Fresh courgette seedlings make a very tasty meal for slugs and snails. If you don't protect your seedlings, then you are likely to lose them all.

There are many ways to protect your plants from these annoying gastropods. You can decide which is best for you. I will go through a few of my favourites.

Slugs and snails will only attack new, soft seedlings. Once your plants get large enough and strong enough, their outer casing will be too hard for the slugs and snails to bite into. Therefore, the slugs and snails won't attack them.

Some of the suggestions for protecting your plants are permanent, but others you will have to keep checking and replace if necessary.

Keeping the garden clear

Slugs and snails like to hide in dark and damp places. So if you keep your growing area free of any dead leaves, tree branches, long grass, and weeds, basically anything they can hide under, this will make it a very unattractive area for them to hang out.

One of their favourite places to hide are under comfrey leaves. So if you want to re-home any slug and snails you find, you can always plant some comfrey in a corner of your garden, and then relocate any you find under the comfrey.

Farmyard friends

If you have chickens, turkeys or ducks, you can always collect any slugs and snails you find and give your birds an occasional afternoon treat. This is a very eco friendly way of disposing of your unwanted gastropods. Don't give them too many as this could cause tummy troubles.

If you have a pond in your garden, try encouraging some frogs to make it their home. Frogs will also eat these pests. And if you are lucky enough to have hedgehogs in your garden, they will also munch their way through a good number of slugs and snails.

Compost heap

If you don't have any of the wonderful slug and snail eating creatures in your garden, you can always collect your slugs and snails and re home them in your compost heap.

> Slugs love compost bins, as there is all sorts of organic matter for them to chew on.

Both slugs and snails are very useful in a compost bin, because they help break everything down. This helps produce the wonderful organic matter we them put back on our garden to feed our plants.

Slugs and snails are only interested in the fresh plant matter that gets put on the compost heap, so will stay near the top of your heap.

I know it's a bit of a shock when you lift the compost bin lid, and you see loads of fat slugs and snails on the underside, but they are doing a good job.

As long as they're happy in your compost bin, they're leaving your plants alone.

Prickly surfaces

Slugs and snails move about on a "foot". It's a muscle that releases mucus to help them move about. They like to move across lovely smooth surfaces, and anything sharp, rough or pointy they don't like, as it hurts their foot.

Around your plants, you can put anything sharp and this should help stop them attacking your plants. Conker shells are useful, so go searching for these when the conkers fall from the trees. You will have to get fresh ones every year because they will rot down.

Mulch

Mulch is a good thing to try. This is very easy to find in local DIY stores and garden centres. Sprinkle a good amount around your plants and the rough surface should help keep slugs and snails away. But it can be expensive.

Wood chips

Wood chips are also a good repellant to try. Hopefully you know someone who can get you some for free. Wood chips are rough and sharp, so they are the slugs' and snails' worst enemy. Sprinkle a good amount round your going seedlings and this should keep these slimy creatures at bay.

Hair

Hair is another good deterrent to try. It doesn't matter if it's pet hair or human hair. I'm not suggesting you shave your entire family's hair off, and then shave the dog and then the cat, but get friendly with your local hairdresser and pooch parlour, as I'm sure they'll have an endless supply for you. Please make sure you explain why you want it first of all, otherwise they may think you're a bit odd.

It doesn't matter what shade the hair is, how long it is, or whether it's tinted or all natural.

> Sprinkle a good amount of hair around your plants and the sharpness of the hair will make it very uncomfortable for even the hardiest of slugs and snails to slide over.

The only downside to using hair is that it's not very tolerant of wind or rain, so you'll have to reapply it regularly.

Coffee grounds

Now I'm not suggesting you start drinking endless cups of coffee, but you should always get friendly with your local coffee shop.

Used coffee grounds from filter coffee are brilliant at keeping slugs and snails off your plants. The smell of the coffee grounds helps repel slugs and snails, but if they do venture onto the coffee grounds, they will find it very difficult to slide over them.

You can use whatever ground coffee you like, but any coffee with caffeine in tends to work better.

Reapply the coffee grounds after rain.

Ash

You can either use ash from a fire place, fire pit, or even a barbecue. But before you put ash round your plants, please make sure that it's completely cold. If you put warm or hot ash round your seedlings, it will burn and kill them.

Don't use ash from a fire that has burned household rubbish, as this may contain toxins that will harm your plants.

Ash is dry, so slugs and snails find it very hard to move across. Scatter liberally around your seedlings, and always replace after wind and rain.

> Ash is great for enriching the soil, so is also a great way to add goodness into the soil for your plants.

Egg shells

If you go through a lot of eggs then this will be perfect for you. If you don't, maybe you can speak to your local sandwich bar, and ask then if you can have all their egg shells? Please explain why you want them first.

Crush the egg shells up a little, making sure the pieces aren't too small. If the shells are too small, they won't work, and the slugs and snails will slither all over them.

Egg shells are sharp and pointy, and make it very painful for slugs and snails to move over them. Scatter a good amount around your seedlings and this should hopefully protect your seedlings from the jaws of these pests.

If you have heavy rain you'll have to reapply.

Grit and sand

This is great one to use, because the sand is too dry for the slugs and snails to slide across, and the grit is too sharp and pointy. This will be very painful for slugs and snails to slide on.

You can find these at your local DIY store, and they are fairly inexpensive.

Liberally scatter around your seedlings and they should be protected from attack. Check regularly, especially after rain, and apply some more if necessary.

Grit and sand doesn't get swept away as quickly as some of the other slug and snail repellants, because it is much heavier, but check it regularly.

Wood shavings

If you are a carpenter, or know someone who is, why not try wood shavings to protect your seedlings?

The texture of sawdust and shavings are both very dry and very rough. If you scatter them liberally around your seedlings, they should help protect them from a slug and snail attack.

Slugs and snails won't like sliding across the wood shavings because it is very painful against their foot.

After strong wind and heavy rain make sure you check the wood shavings, as they may have been blow away. If they have gone then apply some more.

Wood shavings will naturally break down and go into the soil.

Beer

Now this is a very hard one for me, as I love drinking beer. So the thought of buying beer to keep away the slugs and snails is a very tough decision for me. Why waste good beer on these seedling munching monsters?

> Slugs and snails really like beer. So if you want to set beer traps to catch them, either buy the cheapest beer you can find in the supermarket, of if you have any out of date beer in your house use that. We never have out of date beer in our house.

The supermarkets' own brand beer is perfect for slugs and snails.

Setting a beer trap is very easy. All you need are several glass jars, whatever shape or size is fine. Place the glass jars near to your seedlings, or you can dot glass jars all around your garden. Bury most of each jar in the soil, but leave the top inch of each jar showing above the soil.

Slugs and snails love the smell of beer and can't resist having a drink. Fill each jar about half way up with beer and leave your traps ready for those slimy visitors.

Leave over night, and look the following morning. Hopefully you'll find some slugs and snail floating quite happily in an alcoholic stupor.

Remove any victims and put them on your compost bin.

Pellets

I've got to put this in, because it used to be the only way to save your seedlings from being eaten. But, over time, more ways to control slugs and snails have been discovered as I have mentioned above.

But pellets may be the only thing that works for you.

There are various different varieties of pellets available, either online, or in garden centres. Some are much more expensive than others.

You can find biological pellets, some are safe for wildlife (birds and hedgehogs), and pets, but others are not and can have catastrophic consequences. It's always best to read the contents very, very carefully before you buy.

You will only need to sprinkle a few pellets round each seedling when you first plant them outside, or when your seedlings just start to pop through the soil.

Once your plant gets a bit bigger, they will be too large for the slugs and snails to eat.

Pellets can usually survive rain so you won't have to re apply after a shower. The pellets usually start off blue, then go white and fluffy, then dissolve. This can take about 3 weeks.

You will usually only have to put down one lot of pellets round a plant, 3 or 4 usually is enough.

GROWING COURGETTES IN RAISED BEDS OR CONTAINERS

Courgettes can grow very well in raised beds or containers, just make sure you give them enough room to spread out.

Courgette roots don't grow down very far, but do like to spread out and search for water.

Raised beds

Make sure your raised bed is at least 12 inches deep, as this will give your growing plants enough room. Make sure that your raised bed is at least 15 inches wide, but wider if you can. I know this sounds very large, but you have to remember that courgettes spread out as they grow. If you are planting more than one courgette in a raised bed make sure you plant them 24 inches apart from each other.

If you are growing courgettes in containers or raised beds, it may be a good idea to grow a bush variety. I would recommend you try “Eight Ball”.

But if you feel like trying something different, there is a climbing variety of courgette that you can train to climb trellis and this is called “Shooting Star F1”.

Pots

If space is very limited and you can only grow your courgettes in a pot. Make sure the pot is at least 15 inches wide and 12 inches deep.

In the base of the pot put some crocks or large stones as this will help the water drain through. Onto of the stones put a layer of well rotted manure. Fill the remainder of the pot up with multi purpose compost.

Bush varieties are best for growing in pots, so I would recommend you try either “Buckingham F1” or “Endurance F1”.

THE FIRST LEAVES

When your courgette seedlings start to burst through the soil, the first leaves will slowly open.

The first leaves of your courgette plants will look completely different to any of the other leaves that grow.

The first leaves are green and oval in shape. As they open, the leaves will get a little fatter. Then from the centre of these two leaves many more leaves will start to grow. All the other leaves will be sort of circular in shape, but slightly spiky round the edge.

As more leaves grow, the first leaves will turn yellow or brown, shrivel up, and fall off. Don't worry if this happens as this is normal.

The first leaves have some nutrition in them, and once all that is used up, the plant no longer needs them, so it gets rid of them.

POTTING UP YOUR COURGETTE SEEDLINGS

If you sow your courgette seed undercover and only sow one courgette seed per 3 inch pot, you won't need to transplant your growing seedlings into another larger pot before they go outside. They should have enough room in their 3 inch pot for their roots to grow, and the compost should feed them well until it's time for them to go outside.

The larger the seedlings become, the hungrier they will get, so make sure you water them well.

If you have your 3 inch pots in a large seed tray, then you can water your seedlings from the bottom. All you need to do is to pour some water into the tray, making sure it's about 1 inch deep. The roots of your courgette plants will suck up the water. Make sure you don't keep them constantly watered.

When all the water has be absorbed, wait until the top of the compost is a little dry before watering again.

Your courgette seedlings will get quite large, and could make the 3 inch pots topple over, but very soon you will be transplanting them outside into the soil.

TRANSPLANTING YOUR COURGETTES OUTSIDE

If you sowed your courgette seeds undercover, you can transplant them outside into the soil once all fear of frosts have have gone from your area.

Before you transplant your courgette seedlings outside you will need to acclimatise them. Remember they have been growing in a protected environment, so if you suddenly plant them outside without any warning, they may go into shock, stop growing, and then may die.

You need to start to acclimatise your plants about 10 days before you plan on planting them outside. The best way to do this is to place your plants outside in a sheltered spot in your garden during the day. Then just as it's about to get dark, put your plants back inside overnight.

- This will help toughen your plants up, and slowly they will get used to the outside weather.

- If it pours down with rain during the day, it will be best to keep your plants inside.
- Once your plants have acclimatised for 10 days, you can plant them outside in the soil.

You will need to plant your courgette plants at least 2 feet apart from each other. This may seem like a long way, but remember they will spread a great deal and cover most of the bare soil.

- Using a trowel, dig a hole slightly wider and deeper than the pot your courgette seedling has been growing in.
- Put some water in the bottom on the hole you have made, and wait for it to drain away.

Be very careful when getting the courgette seedling out of its pot. Don't pull the plant out because you will break it. Instead, hold the plant carefully between your fingers, turn the plant upside down, tap the bottom of the pot, and remove the pot.

You may find that the roots have poked through the drainage holes of the pot. If they have, be very careful when removing the pot.

Once you have removed the pot, then place the courgette seedling the right way up in the hole you dug. Fill in any remaining space around the seedling with soil. Push the soil down firmly and make sure the soil is level.

Once your courgette plants are in the soil, water around the base of the plants using a watering can with a rose attachment. Watering will fill in any spaces with soil, and will also level off the soil on the top.

You will need to protect your seedling from slugs and snail. I have already made lots of suggestions, so choose which one works best for you.

You will only have to protect your plants from being eaten when you first plant your courgettes out. Once the plants get established and grow bigger, they will be too large for slugs and snails to eat. Also the stems of the plants will develop small prickly spines that will keep these slimy pests at bay.

MALE AND FEMALE FLOWERS

For a courgette plant to produce fruits, it needs both male and female flowers. The pollinators buzz from the male flowers to the female flowers moving the pollen into the stigma. This is how the plant reproduces.

The outside of the courgette flowers look exactly the same, but they aren't. If you look carefully you will see the differences between them.

Male flowers

The male flowers extend from a long thin green stem. This stem can be 4-5 inches long. If you look very carefully inside the male flowers, you will see a short yellow stalk and on top of that there will be a large blob of orange pollen.

Female flowers

The female flowers are on a very short green stem, which is only about 1 inch long. Inside the female flowers you will find the stigma which looks like a bobbly, yellow, circular, fuzzy ring.

Once the pollinators have done their work and moved the pollen to the stigma, then a baby courgette will start to grow below the female flower.

HOW TO LOOK AFTER YOUR COURGETTES AS THEY GROW

Courgettes are very easy to look after, but you need to give them a little helping hand so they can reach their full potential.

Weeding

It is very important to keep the weeds at bay around your courgettes. Weeds grow very fast, and can rapidly cover your courgette plants. If this happens your plants will suffocate and die.

Weeds also create cover for slugs and snails to hide under, and we know what damage they can do.

In order for your courgette plants to produce lots of fruits, the flowers will need to be pollinated by the bees and other insects. If you don't control the weeds around your courgette plants, then the flowers will not open, and therefore the pollinators will not be able to do their work, and you won't get any fruits.

Weed around your courgettes plants once a week. Making sure

you pull out as much of the weed as you can, especially the roots. If you weed regularly then you will stop the weeds spreading, and any weeds that you do grow will only be very small, and will be easy to remove.

Watering

Courgettes are very thirsty plants, so you must make sure you water regularly.

If you sow your seeds directly into the soil, water as soon as you sow your seeds. Use a watering can with a rose attachment. At this early stage only water once a week.

Once the courgette seedlings begin to emerge from the soil, continue watering with a watering can and a rose, but water twice a week.

When the courgette seedlings get established in the soil you should continue to water twice a week, but you will be able to water your plants without the rose attachment on the end of the watering can spout.

If you sow your courgette seeds undercover and transplant outside, make sure you water your plants as soon as you plant them outside in the soil.

You will need to water your plants twice a week as they grow. Only water each plant a little, but as the plants grow larger you'll have to increase the amount of water you give them. If you have a heat wave, you may have to water 3 times a week.

Always water from the base of the plant and use a watering can without a rose on the end. This way the water will get straight down to the roots of the plant, and not sit on the surface of the soil and evaporate away. Try not to get any water on the leaves, as this will cause the leaves to burn during very hot weather and could also cause powdery mildew.

Feeding

Courgette plants are very hungry plants and to help them grow strong and healthy they will benefit from regular feeding.

There are many different plant feeds available either online, or at garden centres. you must always ready the instructions on the box or bottle as they all vary.

Plant feed comes in a variety of different ways, from general plant liquid feed that you mix with water, pellet feed that you scatter on the soil and lightly fork in, dust feed that you sprinkle on the soil and mix in, or granules that you sprinkle on the soil and they slowly release their nutrition.

I prefer to use Shropshire Seaweed fertiliser, because it is full of all sorts of vitamins and minerals from nitrogen, potassium and magnesium. This is only available online, and I've been using it for many years, and it works wonderfully every year.

PESTS AND DISEASES

Powdery mildew

Powdery mildew is a fungal disease and is very common on courgette leaves and stems. If your courgette plant contracts this disease you will notice that the leaves and stems of your courgettes turn white all over. It is more common during the summer as the weather gets much hotter and drier.

If you allow your courgette plants to dry out too much and don't give them sufficient water, they will become stressed and powdery mildew will attack them.

There are chemical sprays that can be used if your plants get powdery mildew, but how effective they are I cannot really say as I worry about the chemicals getting on the fruits and then eating them.

Prevention is the best cure for powdery mildew. Make sure you keep your plants well watered, especially during a very hot summer.

You can mulch around the base of your plants, as this will stop any water evaporating away from surface of the soil.

You can also use any well rotted organic matter around the base of you plants, this will feed your plants as well as retaining moisture in the soil.

When you do water your plants, always use a watering can without a rose attachment on the end. Water at the very base of the courgette plant so the water goes directly into the soil and down to the roots.

And also make sure that you give your plants enough room to spread out. Don't grow your plants too close together as this will help spread the disease from plant to plant.

If you do notice any of your leaves have contracted powdery mildew, remove immediately and throw away. Do not put them in the compost heap. Hopefully if you remove any diseased leaves then the remainder of the plant should be alright.

Courgette rot

This will happen to some of your courgettes, and although it sounds bad, it is nothing to really worry about. It is likely to happen to a couple of your courgettes which is why I thought I would mention it.

You will notice that your courgette fruits will be growing really well, and you'll be very excited when you see the first baby courgettes appear. Then one day, you may notice that 1 or 2 have gone yellow or brown and very soft.

If this happens remove the affected fruits and put them in the compost heap. Leave the other courgettes to continue to grow.

Usually this only happens when the courgettes are really small, but occasionally it will also happen when the courgettes are a little larger. Sometimes the end of a courgette will start to go soft, but the rest of the fruit will be fine. If this does happen, harvest the affected one, cut off the soft end and discard and then you can eat the other part.

Why this happens? Well, it's one of those mysteries. It's not a disease or fungus. It may be the plant's way of getting rid of any excess fruits. But if it does happen, don't panic.

WHEN TO HARVEST YOUR COURGETTES

Courgettes are ready to harvest from mid July and will go on producing fruits until the middle of October.

Courgettes are "tender crops", which means they don't like frost. If you do get a frost in early October, the leaves and stems of your courgette plants will go droopy and the plant will stop producing fruit and die.

You can start to harvest your courgette when they are as small as 3 inches long. Usually most people tend to wait until the courgettes grow a little bit larger. The flower on the end of the courgette will start to shrivel and may fall off.

Don't let your courgettes grow too large, as they will become bitter, watery, and not as tasty.

I would recommend you harvest your courgettes before they get any longer than about 6 inches long, and they should be about an inch and a half in diameter.

When harvesting round courgettes it's best to check what size they recommend on the packet, as they differ.

If you are growing "Eight Ball F1", they should be harvested when they are about the size of a snooker/pool ball which is about 2 inches in diameter.

The variety "Tondo di Piacenza" can grow a little larger before you harvest them. You can allow these to grow to about 3 inches in diameter.

You can let "Floridor f1" courgettes grow even larger. It's best to harvest this variety when they are between 4-6 inches in diameter.

Harvest your courgettes every couple of days, because this will encourage your plants to produce a continuous supply of fruits throughout the summer. Courgettes can either be chopped into large pieces and roasted, sliced and fried, cut in half and stuffed then roasted, the list goes on.

HOW TO HARVEST YOUR COURGETTES

Harvesting your courgettes is very easy, but you must be careful so you don't damage the plant.

Some people twist off their courgettes from the plant, but I find this can damage the plant and other developing fruits. I harvest mine using a small, sharp vegetable knife.

Choose the courgette you are going to harvest, and hold it firmly in one hand and in your other hand hold your knife. Using the blade of the knife very carefully slice through the section where the courgette fruit joins the rest of the plant. Your knife will cut through this section very easily.

Make sure you don't cut any of the main stem of the plant as this could allow diseases to get into the plant.

Harvest as many courgettes as you need.

Check your plant every couple of days to see if you need to harvest any more. Courgette fruits grow fast and the more you harvest, the more the plant will produce.

HOW TO STORE YOUR COURGETTES

Courgettes are best harvested and eaten immediately, but you can store them in the fridge for up to a week. The best way to keep them fresh in the fridge is to store them directly on the shelf. Don't put them in a plastic bag as this will keep them in a moist atmosphere and they will go bad more rapidly.

> I'm not a fan of freezing fresh courgettes, because when you defrost them they go all limp and watery. However, if you have baked a lasagne containing courgettes they seem to freeze quite well.

Preserving

If you have too many courgettes and you don't know what to do with them you can always preserve them.

- You will need to cut your courgettes into chunks and

remove the seeds in the centre. The soft centre will go mushy and won't look very appetising.

- In a saucepan you'll need to add some white wine, vinegar and salt and bring to the boil.
- Once it has boiled, put in the courgettes and leave them to infuse for only five minutes. Make sure you time this, because if you leave them to infuse for any longer, your courgettes will go very mushy.
- Drain the courgettes and allow them to dry.
- In a sterilised jar add some herbs and spices. I like to add thyme, pepper corns, mustard seeds, coriander seeds, fennel seeds and a dried chilli.
- Layer the courgettes on top of the herbs and spice and then cover with olive oil.
- Seal the jar and put in the fridge. They must be eaten within a month.

RECIPE

Sautéed courgettes with feta cheese

Ingredients

- A variety of different courgettes
- 100g Greek Feta, roughly crumbled
- Olive oil
- Salt and pepper

Method

1. Wash the courgettes under cold water to remove any dirt or little prickles.
2. Cut both ends of the courgettes and discard.
3. Chop the courgettes into large 1 inch chunks and put in a large bowl.

4. Sprinkle onto the courgettes some salt and pepper and mix together.
5. Heat a little olive oil in a large frying pan.
6. When the oil is hot add the courgettes.
7. Toss the courgettes in the frying pan until they are a little soft. This should take about 10 minutes.
8. When your courgettes are cooked, tip them into a serving dish, scatter on the crumbled feta and a little more pepper.

FRENCH BEANS

INTRODUCTION

In the UK we call them French beans, but other countries call them haricot vert, green beans, string beans, or snap beans. But, to make things simple, in this book I will refer to them as French beans.

They are native to South America, so don't like frosts or the cold, and hate heavy clay soil. Apart from that they're very easy to grow.

French beans come in two different types, climbing beans or dwarf beans. The bean pods are usually green in colour, but you can also get purple, yellow or even red podded French beans.

The climbing French beans need a structure to climb up, which is usually a bamboo wigwam. Make sure that it is secure in the soil, because the weight of the growing plants and pods could cause your structure to break and fall over in strong winds.

The dwarf French beans are self supporting, so won't need any structure to hold on to. These plants will grow to about 18 inches tall and will be quite bushy.

French bean pods can either be flat, or thin like a pencil. Some pods will grow straight, while others curl up at the end.

Some French bean pods you harvest when they are young and tender, while other French bean pods are left to get mature. The mature pods are harvested when they have dried out and the beans inside are then used in casseroles and stews.

In this chapter I will be looking at the young, tender French beans that you harvest early. I will look at the mature beans in another book.

French beans are what I call "low maintenance", which means that you don't need to do much to them before you cook them. Once you have harvested your French beans, they just need a quick wash and then the very tops of the French beans need to be cut off.

French beans don't need to be topped and tailed, have their side strings removed, or be sliced thinly, unlike some other beans.

VARIETIES OF FRENCH BEANS - DWARF OR CLIMBING

Deciding which type of French beans to grow depends how much room you have, as well as which ones you prefer to eat.

Dwarf French beans

Dwarf French beans only grow to about 18 inches tall, so if you are very limited on space these would be a good choice. They don't need supporting, so if you have a few small raised beds you can plant some French bean plants in one corner of a raised bed.

Dwarf French beans come in a variety of colours, but my favourite are Purple Teepee from Mr Fothergill's Seeds, and Tendergreen from Victoriana Nursery Gardens. Both these dwarf French beans are heavy croppers, which means that they produce a huge amount of beans. They'll both freeze very well, but will lose their colour slightly if they are cooked from frozen rather than from fresh.

Climbing French beans

These will grow very tall, and you will need to create a structure for them to climb up.

You can either use bamboo canes to make a wigwam, or you can make a long bamboo structure called a ridge support instead. You can also use hazel sticks as these are strong, and also bendy. The distance between each cane should be about 6 inches.

You can also use trellis, an arch, or even netting. But make sure that whatever you use, it is strong and firm enough to take the weight of your growing beans.

Your French bean plants will get very heavy as they grow, and if your structure isn't sturdy enough, it will fall over, and you won't be able to get it back up again.

If you are growing your climbing French beans in a small raised bed in your garden, or on your patio, the best way is to grow them up a small wigwam. Wigwams don't take up much space, and you can then grow other smaller crops around them.

If you are using sticks as a structure for your climbing French beans, (whether it be bamboo or hazel), you'll need to make sure that they're about 10 foot in length. I know this seems very long, but at least 12 inches your stick needs to go in the soil, and the plants will keep climbing until they don't want to climb any more.

The climbing French beans that I would recommend are Cobra from Mr Fothergill's Seeds, Blue Lake from Victoriana Nursery Gardens, or Cherokee Trail of Tears from Pennard Plants.

These will all give you an excellent crop and all of them taste wonderful.

PREPARING THE SOIL

Whether you are growing dwarf or climbing French beans, they will grow in practically any type of soil. Although, if you have heavy clay soil, then they may struggle, and also they may not do very well in soil that is too acidic.

Thoroughly dig over the area where you are going to plant your French beans, using a large garden fork. This will open up the soil, and allow oxygen to get into the soil. Remove any weeds and break up any large clumps of earth.

Once this is done, spread a thin layer of well rotten horse manure on top of the soil and fork it in well.

The manure makes the soil lovely and rich, which the beans will love.

What I remember my mum and granddad doing when they were going to plant their French beans, was to dig a trench. Many people still do this. Digging a trench will only work if you are growing your French beans up a ridge support.

Digging a trench needs to be done in March. Your trench should be about 12 inches deep, and about 12 inches wide, but as long as your ridge support is going to be.

When you dig out the soil to make your trench, leave the soil heaped next to your trench. You will need to put this soil back in your trench before you put your structure up.

Over the course of the next couple of months, fill your trench with grass cuttings, vegetable peelings (not potato peelings as they will sprout), apple cores, banana skins, tea bags, coffee grounds, and torn up newspaper. All these will break down and feed your French bean plants as they grow.

Do make sure that every night you cover the trench with chicken wire or plastic, anything to stop the foxes from digging at it during the night.

I forgot to cover mine up once, and came back to the allotment the following day and the foxes had dug everything out over night and there were vegetable peelings and left over fruit everywhere.

Keep filling your trench up with all these goodies until the middle of May, when you'll then need to fill the remainder of the trench with the soil you removed in March.

Once you have filled up your trench with the soil, give it a firm pat down and then it's ready for putting in your canes to make your structure.

WHEN AND HOW TO SOW YOUR FRENCH BEANS - INSIDE AND OUT

French beans are tender crops, which means they don't like the cold. Frost will kill your French beans, so please don't be in any hurry to get them outside. Check the last frost date for your area, and, a couple of weeks prior, keep your eyes on your local weather, because if the weather is going to be mild and calm, you may be able to plant your French beans outside earlier.

I live in the southeast of England, and my last frost date is 31st May, but sometimes I can get mine out a little earlier.

This is how I sow my French bean seeds, you may have to adjust your timings a little.

I have tried sowing my French bean seeds straight out in the soil, as well as starting them off in a greenhouse, and I find that I get better results when I start my French bean seeds off inside my greenhouse first.

If you don't have a greenhouse, then a sunny window sill will work just as well.

SOWING INSIDE

Sow your French bean seeds four weeks before your last frost date. So for me I'll sow my French bean seeds at the beginning on May, because I can transplant mine outside from the beginning of June.

Get a 3 inch pot and fill it nearly to the top with multi purpose compost. Gently pat the compost down, but make sure you don't compress it too firmly.

You can sow two French bean seeds per 3 inch pot, as there is plenty of room. Place one seed on one side and another seed on the other, I say one north and one south.

Push the seeds into the soil about 1 inch and then cover them over with some more compost.

If you are growing your French bean seeds in smaller pots, then only sow one seed per pot.

Once you have sown all the seeds you want, water them from above. The reason I water from above is so that any excess water can trickle through the drainage holes in the bottom of the pots. If your bean seeds sit in water, they will go mouldy and won't grow.

Only water again when the compost is a little on the dry side.

After about a week, your beans should start to push their way through the compost and you'll see them.

As with most seeds, not all will germinate, so make sure you sow a few extra seeds just in case.

As the shoots appear they will be attacked by slugs and snails, so make sure you protect your plants from them. There are many ways of doing this, from pellets, coffee grounds, pet hair, and egg shells.

My favourite way, to control these slippery pests, is to give them to my chickens. Chickens love slugs and snails. If you don't have chickens, then get friends and family to save all their egg shells for you. Crush the egg shells up fairly small, and sprinkle around your plants. The slugs and snails find egg shells sharp and uncomfortable, so will stay away.

SOWING OUTSIDE

You can sow French bean seeds straight out in the soil.
For climbing French beans, you must have your structure in place first before you sow your French bean seeds, so decide whether you're going to make wigwam or a ridge support.

Make sure the soil is weed free and any large lumps of soil are broken down.

For dwarf French beans, sow a pair of seeds together about 2 inches deep, making sure you cover them with soil. Then leave a space of about 12 inches before you sow the next pair of seeds. This will give the growing plants plenty of room to grow, and if you find that both seeds germinate, you can either, take out the weakest seedling, or leave both seedlings to grow together.

The best time to sow your French bean seeds outside is two weeks

before your last frost date, so for the southeast of England where I live, I would sow mine in the middle of May.

For climbing French beans, plant three seeds round each cane of your structure, evenly spaced apart from each other.

Push each seed into the soil about two inches. This is deeper than if you are sowing them inside, because they will need more protection from the weather as they start to grow.

Cover your seeds with a little more soil.

Whether you've sown climbing of dwarf French beans, make sure that you water them in well, and once the water has drained away from the surface of the soil, put down some protection from the slugs and snails. Once the shoots start to appear above the soil they will be very tasty to any passing slugs and snails.

Your French bean shoots should start to appear above the soil in about two weeks, just as all worries of frost are gone from your area.

I tend to find that the germination rate is poorer when sowing French beans straight out in the soil, so I tend to opt for starting mine off inside.

WHAT DO THE FIRST LEAVES LOOK LIKE?

The first, or baby leaves that you will see, don't look like all the rest of the leaves that will form as your French beans grow.

The baby leaves are long, oval, and green. It is the bean seed that has split in half lengthways. These will then usually shrivel and fall off.

All the other leaves that form after the baby leaves will start small, and gradually grow larger as the plant grows larger.

WHEN TO PLANT YOUR FRENCH BEANS OUTSIDE

Remember French beans are tender crops, which means they don't like the cold weather, and even if you have a very light frost it will kill them, and you'll have to start again.

So before you plant your French beans outside, make sure you know when the last frost date in your area is.

If you have been growing your seedlings in a greenhouse, they have been protected from wind and rain, so they must be acclimatised before being moved outside. If you don't acclimatise your plants, they will have a massive shock, get stressed, and stop growing.

Acclimatising your plants is very important but very easy to do. All it means is getting them used to the outside world gradually, and this toughens them up.

About ten days before you're planning on planting your French bean seedlings outside, and only if the weather is fairly calm and warm, bring your seedlings out of the greenhouse, and leave them outside in a protected area of your garden all day.

As the temperature gets cooler before the sun sets, place your seedlings back in your greenhouse overnight. Bring your seedlings out each day, and this will make moving them into the soil much easier and less stressful on the plant.

When you plant your French bean seedings outside, they should be about 9-12 inches tall. This is the perfect size as they're still able to stand up on their own and haven't started to curl up with each other.

Plant two seedlings around each bamboo cane. I find that two plants is perfect, they have plenty of room each and they don't get over crowded.

Dig a hole in the soil, as close to your bamboo cane as you can. Make sure the bean plants sit a little lower in the soil than they did in the pot.

When removing your French bean plants from their pot, place one hand over the top of the pot, making sure you carefully hold the bean plants between two of your fingers. Tip the pot upside down, and give it a pat, this releases the soil and the roots from inside the pot. You will now be able to lift off the pot. Place the French bean seedlings carefully in the hole you have dug in the soil.

Fill around the French bean seedlings with soil, and firm the soil around it. Take care not to break the delicate stems of the French bean plants.

Once all your French bean plants are in the soil, water them, and then protect the tender little plants from slugs and snails.

HOW TO LOOK AFTER YOUR FRENCH BEANS AS THEY GROW

French beans don't really take much looking after. But there are a few things that you must do.

As your climbing French bean plants grow they *should* wind themselves around the nearest bamboo cane. But sometimes they have other ideas. So keep an eye on your plants, and if any of your French bean plants find this difficult, all you have to do is give them a helping hand.

Using a small piece of garden string, attach the growing French bean plant to its nearest cane.

This should only need to be done when the climbing French bean plants are small. Once the plants get established they should then be fine.

Dwarf French beans should grow quite happily and will not need any structure to climb up.

French beans are thirsty plants, especially if the weather is very hot and dry. So water your plants very well, at least twice a week. Add some Shropshire Seaweed fertiliser to your water, as this will help your plants as they grow and give them loads of nutrients.

When the flowers start to bloom, some gardeners spray the

flowers with a fine mist of water from a garden hose. This helps to **set** your flowers.

Setting means the flowers will then produce a baby bean. If your flowers don't **set**, the flower will just fall off and there will be no baby bean growing underneath.

To help your flowers to **set**, you must also make sure you water thoroughly, and add some feed to the water. Also, if you have some spare manure, place that round the bottom of your plants, and harvest your crop regularly.

PESTS AND DISEASES

There are quite a few pests and diseases that your beans can get, but I will mention the most common ones.

Aphids

Aphids, or green and black fly, will suddenly appear. They tend not to cover your entire crop, usually only a couple of plants. Aphids will stop the plant from growing and destroy any leaves and flowers that are developing. Aphids are very easy to get rid of, as long as you catch them early. The most ecologically friendly way is to go and catch as many ladybirds as you can. Ladybirds will eat about 100 aphids a day, but aphids do produce babies very quickly.

If you don't have time to go and find loads of ladybirds, there is something else you can try.

Get a plastic spray bottle, and put in a small squirt of washing up liquid. Fill the rest of the bottle up with cold water. You can then spray this mixture onto your affected plants.

The soap from this mixture blocks up the aphids airways, and they are unable to breath. They die very quickly and simply slip off the plant.

As a bonus your French bean plants will then be very clean.

Another option, and if you have a very heavy infestation, is to go and buy a spray from your local garden centre, I would recommend Bayer Garden Ultimate Bug Killer, it works very well.

If you catch aphids early, then you can use one of the eco friendly ways, before you have to resort to buying a spray.

Powdery mildew

You may find that the leaves on your French beans go white. This is powdery mildew. The best thing to do is to harvest what French beans you can from the affected plant, and then remove the affected stems and either burn them, or take them to your local recycling centre.

Do not put them in your compost heap, because you will spread the disease.

To stop this from happening, make sure you grow your beans in a different place every year, and allow the air to circulate well around the plants.

Downy mildew

The leaves on your French beans may also go yellow in colour. Harvest what beans you can from the plant, and then remove the affected stems and burn them or take them to your local recycling area.

Do not put them in your compost heap.

To prevent this, make sure that you plant your beans in a different place every year and allow the air to circulate round the plants.

At the end of the season when the beans are coming to the end, you will notice that the leaves and stems of **all** the plants will go yellow or light brown. Don't worry about this, as it's just your plants telling you that they've done their work for the year and now they're finished.

Sometimes this is confused with downy mildew

As with all pests and diseases, it's best to try and get them sorted as soon as they appear, so be vigilant and check your plants regularly.

WHEN AND HOW TO HARVEST YOUR FRENCH BEANS

Your French beans will be ready to harvest usually from July and you can continue to harvest them all the way through to September.

When you first harvest them, you will start with just a few, and as long as you pick your French beans regularly, soon you'll be picking loads of them.

You will need to harvest your French beans every couple of days.

You don't have to wait for French beans to get ripe, they are ready to harvest what ever size they are. But the best size to harvest your French beans is when they are about 4-5 inches long. If your French beans get too long, then the sides will get **stringy** and the beans inside the pod will be tough.

You may be wondering what a **stringy** bean is.

It happens when the French bean gets too large and the sides of the bean will then get hard. If you try to eat it, it will be very tough and it will feel like you are trying to eat some pieces of string. Not very nice.

If you find that some of your beans have got too big, don't harvest them. Leave them on the plant, and they will keep swelling up. Eventually the pod will go dry and you can save the seeds to plant the following year.

It's very easy to harvest your French beans. Using one hand, hold the stem just above the French bean you are going to harvest. Then with your other hand, take hold of the French bean, and pull down firmly. The bean should come off very easily.

FRENCH BEAN RECIPE

French beans are very easy to cook, but they can very easily lose their bright colour. Here is a slightly different way in which to cook them. They will keep their wonderful colour and I add a little something special to give them a little bit more flavour.

Ingredients

- French beans
- A little olive oil
- 2 cloves of garlic
- Salt and pepper

Method

1. Get a large saucepan and fill it two thirds full with water, and bring to the boil.

2. Wash your French beans in cold water, and then cut off their tops.
3. When the water in the saucepan starts to boil add a large pinch of salt.
4. Add the French beans to the boiling water all at once, and bring the water back to the boil.
5. Cook the French beans for 2 minutes.
6. Remove the beans from the hot water and immediately put them in cold water. This will stop the beans from cooking any more and will make sure they retain their colour.
7. In a large frying pan heat a little olive oil gently on a low heat.
8. Cut the cloves of garlic into very thin slices, or chop finely and add to the oil.
9. Drain the French beans, and add them to the oil and garlic in the frying pan.
10. Toss the French beans to coat them in the garlic and oil, and add a little salt and pepper.
11. After a couple of minutes the beans will be heated through and will be ready to serve.

ONIONS

INTRODUCTION

I don't know about you, but I use onions in practically every savoury recipe I cook. They are the building blocks to most soups, casseroles, stews and curries.

They can be fried, roasted, sautéed, and even boiled. They can be stuffed in chickens or turkeys, and their flavour can permeate through the meat as it cooks.

On Bonfire night when you need to keep warm whilst watching fireworks, caramelised onions are perfect with a good quality sausage in some french bread.

Onions are from the Allium family which also includes shallots, garlic, leeks and chives. They come in a lovely variety of colours from white, brown, yellow, light pink, to dark red.

They are very easy to grow and although they have a reputation for making you cry when you cut them, please don't let that put you off. Some are mild in flavour and others are quite strong and pungent.

They can be eaten raw in salads, although if the slices are too large, they may make your eyes water if the onions have a very strong flavour. I personally prefer cooking them slowly to release their natural sugars.

DIFFERENT TYPES OF ONIONS

The best way to grow onions is by buying **sets**. These are very small versions of onions and are usually **heat treated** so they won't **bolt** (go to seed) in the hot weather. I will explain more about these terms a little later on.

You can sow your onions from **seed**, but they do take longer and they are more likely to bolt during the hot summer.

Onions come in two different types: **spring planting** onions and **autumn planting** onions. So make sure that you get the right ones for the time when you want to plant them.

In the south of the UK, where I live, I sow my **spring planting** onions outside from **mid March to late March**, then they're ready to harvest about **July to August** of the same year.

Whereas the **autumn planting** ones I'll plant in **September to October** time and they'll grow slower over the winter and then be ready to harvest to harvest **June or July** the following year.

So, hopefully you can see that the spring planting onions grow much quicker, but their flavour may not be as mature. Whereas the autumn planting onions take much longer to grow but will have a more rounded mature flavour.

VARIETIES OF ONIONS

Choosing which variety of onions you wish to grow is quite a tricky business. Some are small and others are large, so it just depends what size onions you want to grow.

Do you want small onions to roast whole, or will you be slicing them to put in some wonderful pasta dishes?

I personally prefer the larger onions and the varieties that I tend to grow every year are: **Centurion**, **Hercules**, and **Stuttgarter giant**, these are all white onions and the red onions I grow are **Red Baron.**

You can find loads of fantastic varieties online, both sets and seeds, at **Thompson & Morgan, Mr Fothergill's Seeds,** and **Victoriana Nursery Gardens.** Or pop into your local garden centre where they usually have a good selection, or even your local DIY store. They may only have a few varieties to choose from but they're usually very good.

SEEDS OR SETS

You may be wondering what the difference is when growing your onions from seeds or growing them from sets. Let me explain about each of these.

Seeds

Well, you know what a seed is, well I hope you do. Onion seeds are easily bought from online retailers or in a garden centre. When growing onions from seed they take much longer.

You must sow the seeds in January.

Fill a seed tray, nearly to the top with some multipurpose compost. Moisten the compost and then sprinkle the seeds on top of the compost, making sure that none of the seeds are touching each other.

Cover the seeds with a little more compost and then place the tray in a warm environment (a sunny window sill is perfect).

Once the seedlings get to about 3-4 inches tall, transplant each one into a small pot full of fresh compost and then give them a water.

Keep your onion seedlings in a warm place as they continue to grow a little larger and make sure you water them when the soil gets dry.

By the time you get to early March, the weather should be much warmer, so your onion seedlings can be moved into a greenhouse or cold frame. At night, place a propagator lid over your onion seedlings, but during the day remove the propagator lid to let the air circulate.

Then, from about the little of March onwards, depending where you live and what the weather decides to do, your seedlings should be ready to be transplanted outside in the garden.

Your onion seedlings should be about 6-8 inches tall by the time you come to plant them outside.

When you transplant your onions outside, make sure that you plant them about 4-6 inches apart from each other and then the rows about 9 inches apart from each other.

Once the seedlings are in the soil, water them in and they should grow beautifully for you.

Sets

Onion sets are basically very small onions and everything that I mentioned above has already been done for you.

When you get your onion sets you can sow them straight out into the soil from the middle to the end of March. Again you may have to adjust your timings due to where you live and the weather.

Onion sets can be bought online at the big seed companies, and they always have some wonderful varieties, but you can also buy onion sets in garden centres. They won't have as many varieties to choose from, usually only the most popular ones.

Once you get your onion sets home, don't leave them in the bag they come in. Remove them immediately as they'll sweat and then go mouldy.

Empty your onions sets out onto a metal tray and sort through each and every one.

Get rid of any that have got the slightest bit of mould on them, or are soft. Discard them as they won't grow.

I start my onion sets off early, to give them a bit of a head start. Let me tell you how I do that.

STARTING YOUR ONION SET OFF EARLY

Why do I start my onions off early? Well, for a few reasons:

Firstly, when I first get mine, it's too cold outside to plant them. If I leave them for too long without planting them in soil, they'll all go mouldy.

Secondly, starting them off early means that when the weather is warm enough to plant them outside in the ground, my onions already have a lovely green shoots growing at the top, and a lovely set of roots growing at the bottom. With both the shoots and roots growing, the onions will establish themselves much faster in the soil.

When you come to plant them outside in the soil, if you see that any haven't grown, then you can just discard them because if they've not done anything now then they won't do anything at all.

Here's how I start mine off:

All you need to do is get a lovely sturdy seed tray.

Then get some cardboard toilet rolls. Ask friends and family if they can save their toilet rolls for you throughout the year as well, but please explain why you want them, you don't want them thinking that you have a strange toilet roll fetish.

Using a good pair of scissors, cut each toilet roll in half, crossways, so each roll makes two small cylinders.

Stand each cylinder up, and fit as many into the seed tray as you can. There should be about twenty eight in total (4 across and 7 down).

Then fill each cylinder with compost, but don't pack it in too tightly.

Once each cylinder is full of compost, take the onions and place one onion in each cylinder, making sure the roots are touching the soil.

Push each onion down into the compost about 1 inch.

When each cylinder has one onion in it, then water in well.

The seed tray can then be left in your greenhouse or cold frame until you're ready to plant your onions outside in the soil.

Water when the soil is dry, but don't over water. Little and often is the key.

PLANTING YOUR ONIONS OUTSIDE

Let me start off with onion sets.

If you don't want to, or can't, start your onions sets off early in a greenhouse or cold frame, then you can plant them straight outside in the soil.

For **white, brown or yellow onions**, these can be planted outside as soon as the soil is warm enough. In the south of the UK, onions can usually be planted in the soil from the middle of March. But, if you are still having hard frosts which make the soil far to hard to dig, then leave planting them for a couple of weeks.

Make sure that all your white, brown and yellow onions are planted out by the middle of April at the very latest.

If you live in a cooler climate then your onion sets will need to be planted out a couple of weeks later. Or you could plant them out at the time I suggest, but just make sure you put a cloche or small poly tunnel over the top of your onions to help keep some heat in.

When you plant your white, brown or yellow onion sets out in the soil, make sure the onions are approximately 4-6 inches apart from each other, and that the rows are 6 inches apart That way the onions have plenty of room to spread their roots, and also for their bulbs to swell up as they grow.

If you are growing **red onions**, then these need to be planted out a little later, as they need the soil to be even warmer.

Again for the south of the UK, I will plant mine in the middle of April, but make sure they are all in by the end of April. These also will need to be planted about 4-6 inches apart and the rows 6 inches apart.

If you have started your onion sets off early in a greenhouse or cold frame, then you will need to **harden off** your onions before you plant them outside.

What is **hardening off**, I hear you say? Well, you'll hear it a lot when you're growing your plants. What it means is slowly getting your seedlings or small plants used to the big outside world. Remember they have been growing in a protected area since you sowed them, and haven't been exposed to the wind, rain, and sudden changes in temperature. So you need to get them used to this.

HOW TO HARDEN OFF YOUR ONIONS

During the day, if it is a calm day, bring your onions out of your greenhouse or cold frame and place them in a protected area of your garden. On your patio, for example.

Leave your onions out all day so they can soak up the sun's rays and feel the breeze between their shoots.

Then, just before it gets dark, put your onions back in your greenhouse or cold frame again to keep them protected from the cold weather at night.

Do this for ten days, and then your plants will become more robust.

If you don't harden off your onions, and plant them straight out in the open soil, your onions will panic, become stressed, stop growing, and could possibly die.

I like to think of it like a baby growing into a toddler, then into a small child and finally into a big child. You start them off in a cot, and as they grow you gradually move them into a smaller bed, and then when they grow even bigger, you move them into a larger bed.

If you have sown your **onions from seed** and have been growing them in a greenhouse or cold frame, you will also need to harden off your onion plants before you transplant them outside.

Do them exactly the same way as I have just mentioned. The best time to transplant your onion seedlings outside is in early April to the middle of April.

You can of course sow your **onion seeds straight out into the soil.** If you are going to do that, then they can be sown throughout March.

You will need to dig the soil and remove any weeds and large stones.

Make a shallow trough in the soil about one inch deep and as long as you want.

Water the trough and allow the water to drain away before sowing your onion seeds.

If you are planting several rows of onion seeds, make sure the rows are about 6 inches apart from each other.

Sprinkle your onion seeds in the trough very thinly and then carefully cover them over with some more soil and gently pat the soil down.

Label clearly, and place a stick at each end of your row, so you know where it begins and ends.

After a few days, water carefully using a rose on the end of a watering can, unless you have had a decent amount of rain.

Keep the area round the growing onions weed free.

As the onions grow you will need to thin them out, so that the onions are about 4 inches apart from each other.

RED ONIONS OR WHITE ONIONS

Now to be honest, it's all really down to personal preference. There is a difference in flavour between red and white onions, and it just depends what you prefer.

Red onions have a sweeter flavour to them, and aren't as strong. They are great in salads, and I like roasting them with chicken pieces, lemon, and garlic. They also go very well together in my red onions & potato rosti recipe.

White onions have a much stronger flavour and are used as the basis of most dinners that I cook at home. They can also be roasted and this softens their harsh flavour and brings out their sweetness.

I like roasting a variety of onions with some olive oil, salt & pepper, and then adding some fried pancetta and parmesan cheese onto the top. This makes a lovely change to the usual vegetables that you tend to have with dinners.

They go especially well with some great quality sausages, mashed potato, and gravy. My recipe for roasted onions with pancetta and parmesan can be found near the end of the book.

HOW TO LOOK AFTER YOUR ONIONS AS THEY GROW

To help your onions grow really well, you will need to keep them weed free. Be very careful when weeding around them, and make sure you don't damage the growing bulbs with your tools. If you do, then this could possibly allow disease to get into the growing bulb, and it may go mouldy and die.

Make sure you water your onions well, especially through the dry months. Onions need water to help them grow. And if you have a prolonged heatwave and your onions don't get enough water, the plants will get stressed, and their growth will either slow down, or stop completely.

They are also very hungry plants, so feed them with a liquid fertiliser about once a week, I use Shropshire Seaweed Fertiliser and they love it.

You may also notice that sometimes your onions start **bolting.** Sometimes this is called **going to seed.**

If your onions do **bolt**, all it means is that they're trying to reproduce.

How will you know if your onions are **bolting?** What will you see? A long green stem will grow from the middle of your onion and will grow up quite high. On top of the green stem you'll see a round section appear, this will turn into very pretty flower head with lots of very small flowers on it. The bees will love these flowers and if you leave the flowers on, you'll have loads of buzzing visitors. Then, once the flowers have died, the seeds will appear.

If you do see this happen, don't panic. Just cut off the shoot at its base, and then the onion will then carry on putting all its effort into growing bigger and bigger, and not putting all its effort into making lots of seeds.

If you have grown your onions from **sets**, then these are usually **heat treated**, which is a process that many seed companies use. This helps to prevent the growing onions from **bolting,** and also extends the growing period of the onions so that you get a better harvest.

If you are growing your onions from **seeds** then these aren't usually **heat treated**, so the likelihood of these **bolting** is quite high.

Make sure your onions get enough water, especially during the summer months, as this will also help stop them from bolting. But, if they do, just follow the instructions above.

PESTS AND DISEASES

Onions can suffer from an array of problems, and I will just mention a few of the most common problems that I usually encounter.

Onion fly

Oh, the dreaded onion fly. I say this with dismay.

There is a very eco-friendly way of dealing with this and that is to alternate one row of onions with one row of carrots.

The reason for this is because the smell from the carrots deters the onions fly, and the smell from the onions deters the carrot fly.

It's brilliant, plants working together to help each other out.

I alternate my onions and carrots every year and it works brilliantly. The onion fly is usually a problem in the summer when the soil is dry.

The onion fly maggots will burrow into the bottom of the onion bulb and basically eat it from the inside out. Yuck! They are very small and white. Once they have finished with one, then they'll go onto another one.

You will know when your onions have onion fly, because the leaves of your onions will start to go yellow and droop over.

If you do discover you have this, then lift the infected plants and burn them. **Do not** put them in the compost heap.

To prevent onion fly from from attacking your onions, try firming up the soil around the base of each onion and grow your onions from sets rather than seeds.

Neck rot

Neck rot may occur during the storage of the onion bulb.

The way to stop this is to make sure that when you harvest your onions allow them to dry out fully.

This must be done in a single layer in a greenhouse, shed or garage. I will talk more about harvesting and drying out in the next chapter.

If your onions aren't dried out enough before you store them, they may sweat and get hot. This will cause mould to grow and very quickly your entire onion crop will rot.

If you do notice that any of your onions are going mouldy in storage, then you must remove them immediately otherwise the mould will spread to the neighbouring onions.

Rust

Rust is fairly uncommon when growing onions, but rust can also affect leeks, and garlic in much the same way.

You know when your onions have rust because you will see some small orange patches appear on the leaves.

Rust usually appears from mid-summer to late autumn. Usually, you would have harvested all your onions by then, which is why it is quite rare for your onions to get it. If you do find rust on your onion leaves, remove any affected leaves immediately. Just cut off the affected leaves and either burn them, or take them to your local recycling centre. Do not put them on your compost heap, because this will allow the disease to spread.

Then you must make sure that you do not grow your onions in the same area for a couple of years.

There are of course many other pests and diseases, but I have just mentioned the ones that are more common.

For more information and other diseases, please refer to the RHS Website: https://www.rhs.org.uk/science/plant-health-in-gardens/entomology

WHEN TO HARVEST AND DRY OUT YOUR CROP

Your onions will be ready to harvest in about August time, obviously this will differ slightly if you live in a hotter or cooler climate.

How to know when your onions are ready to harvest. Firstly the leaves will droop over and then will lose all their green colour and go brown. Once this happens your onions will no longer grow any larger.

You can then either leave them to sunbathe in the sunshine for a couple of weeks before you carefully dig them up, or, if you are due heavy rain, harvest them all immediately and place them in a greenhouse, garage or shed to dry out.

To dig your onions up, just use a trowel or a small hand fork and gently dig the soil around your onions and they should come up very easily.

You need to make sure your onions dry out very thoroughly before you store them, because if they aren't dried out properly, then some of the onions may go mouldy and rot and then the rotted ones will rot any that are around them, and before you know it, you'll lose your entire harvest.

When drying out your onions, make sure that they are in one layer and are on a wire rack so that the air can circulate around them.

Once you have harvested your onions you can use them immediately in cooking, but check each one every week, and if you find any damaged ones use immediately.

Leave your onions to dry out for at least 4 weeks, maybe longer if you can. You'll know when you onions are dried out enough, because a few of the outer layers of the onion skin will be papery and dry.

Once your onions are dried out you can either place them in a fabric bag or if you're very clever you can plait them. I'm not very good at doing that (or have the patience), so I just put them in a fabric bag.

ONION RECIPE

Roasted onions with pancetta and parmesan

Onions are the basis for many recipes, but they can also stand alone as a vegetable themselves.

Here is one way that I like to cook mine. Roasting onions brings out their sweetness and the pancetta brings a little saltiness to the dish. Adding a sprinkling of parmesan on top right at the end just lifts it to new heights.

Ingredients

- A selection of red and white onions
- A little olive oil
- Salt and pepper
- Pancetta, cubed
- Shaved parmesan cheese

Method

1. Set your oven to gas mark 5, 190 C, or 375 F.
2. Get your onions and peel them, but leave the root on as this holds the onion together. If you have any stray roots trim those off.
3. If you onions are small, then cut your onions into 4 even pieces, but if they are large cut into 8. Make sure that you cut through the root.
4. Place your onion pieces on a baking tray in one even layer. Sprinkle over some olive oil, salt & pepper, and then mix with your hands to make sure every piece of onion is coated.
5. Place on the middle shelf of the oven and cook for about 30 minutes, or until the onions are soft and the edges of the onions have started to crisp up.
6. While the onions are cooking in the oven, get a large frying pan, and pour in a little more olive oil and add the cubed pancetta. Cook the pancetta until it has turned a lovely golden brown colour.
7. Using a slotted spoon, remove the cooked pancetta from the frying pan, and place on some kitchen towel to drain away any excess fat. Make sure you leave any fat in the frying pan as you'll need that later.
8. Once the onions come out of the oven, let them cool for a few minutes before placing them in the same frying pan and immediately add the pancetta.
9. Toss both the onions and pancetta together carefully for just a few minutes, and then serve.
10. Sprinkle a little shaved parmesan on top for extra flavour.

POTATOES

INTRODUCTION

Potatoes have been around for thousands and thousands of years, possibly since about 8,000 BC. They didn't arrive in Europe until the 16th Century and disaster struck in 1845 when blight caused the crops to fail, which led to the Irish Potato Famine.

But potatoes recovered and we now grow an astonishing amount of them every year. They are a staple in many diets and are very versatile.

I grow potatoes every year and have tried out many different varieties and I'll let you know which ones I prefer. I'll also let you know how to grow them, how to look after them, what diseases to keep an eye out for, how to harvest them and, finally, how to cook them.

DIFFERENT TYPES OF POTATOES

You may think that a potato is a potato, but no.

There are three standard types of potatoes: **First early**, **second early**, and **main crop.**

You can also get **extra early** potatoes, but these need to be started inside and in warm soil, then moved outside when the temperature is warmer. The extra early potatoes must always be grown in containers.

Let me explain a little about each of these to you:

First early potatoes are usually sown between March to April time. You can then harvest these in June or July. They are the first of the potatoes to be ready. They produce small potatoes that are perfect for using in salads or as new potatoes. The skins don't need peeling as they are very thin, and once they've been harvested they just need a quick wash and then you can boil them with a little mint.

Second early potatoes are also sown between March to April time. You can harvest these in July and August. They are larger than the first early potatoes and can still be boiled with mint, but you'll most probably have to cut these potatoes in half as they will be larger and therefore take longer to cook.

Main crop potatoes can be sown from mid March to mid May. These take longer to grow and you will start harvesting these around September and October time. Main crop potatoes produce very large potatoes that are ideal for baking and roasting.

First and second early potatoes will grow very happily in large containers, but main crop potatoes need much more room, so I would suggest these are grown in the open soil. Obviously if you have some containers that are large enough then by all means use them.

VARIETIES OF POTATOES

There are many varieties of potatoes from each of the first early, second early and main crops, and it's your own personal choice as to which ones you want to grow.

It depends on what you're looking for in a potato: some are floury and soft inside and some are more waxy in texture.

Potatoes will grow in most soils, they're not fussy. Just fork in a good amount of organic matter, like well-rotted horse manure, and sprinkle on top of the soil some potato fertiliser and both these will give your potatoes a great start.

Below are some of the varieties I particularly like:

First early potatoes

Arran, Foremost, Pentland Javelin, Red Duke of York and Swift.

Second early potatoes

Kestrel, Nicola and Vivaldi

Main crop potatoes

Apache, Desiree, International Kidney, Maris Piper, King Edward, Picasso and Sarpo Mira

Of course, there are many more to choose from, but these are just my favourites. Some of these potatoes have white skins (Swift), others yellow (Vivaldi), some pink (Sarpo Mira), others light brown and red (King Edward) and some white and red (Apache).

You can get purple and blue potatoes, yes that's right. Shetland Black are purple, but these are only dark purple on the outside and mainly white inside, but then once I grew Blue Danube and they're purple throughout the entire potato.

You're most probably thinking that this sounds quite interesting, and yes they are. But don't mash them, because purple mashed potato on your dinner plate really does look odd. They're perfect cubed and roasted, but please take my advice and don't mash them.

CHITTING

You're most probably wondering what this is. Well all it really means is *letting your seed potatoes sprout*.

When you want to grow potatoes you need to buy **seed potatoes**. These are usually bought in a 1.5 kg bag. These bags can be found online, in DIY stores, or your local garden centre.

Online retailers have more variety, but make sure you order then as soon as possible. They tend to have them on sale from about November time. If you order your seed potatoes online, they'll be sent to you in about January/February time (if you live in the southern hemisphere, sowing times will differ).

Garden centres tend to have their seed potatoes on sale once the New Year starts. Depending on the size of your garden centre, depends on how many varieties they'll have on offer.

DIY stores again will have their seed potatoes on sale in about January, but tend to have a very limited selection.

Where ever you get your potatoes from, make sure that as soon as you get them home you must remove them from their bag. If they're left in their bag they'll sweat and go mouldy, then they're no good to anyone and all you can do then is put them on the compost heap.

Not all potatoes need chitting. First early and second early potatoes don't really need chitting, but, if you want to, it won't do them any harm. Main crop potatoes **must** be chitted.

What I do is to place the potatoes in a single layer on a black seed tray. Make sure that there is some space around them so the air can circulate. I find that one bag weighing 1.5 kg per seed tray is perfect. Make sure you label the trays, then you know which variety is in that tray, and also label whether they're first early, second early or main crop as well.

Once all this is done the trays need to be placed in a frost free environment with easy access to light and good air circulation. If you have a sunny window sill, then that is perfect. I place mine on the top of the kitchen cupboards.

Check on your potatoes once a week, and if there are any seed potatoes that have gone mouldy then remove them and throw them away. You may get one or two but this very rarely happens.

What you want to end up with on your seed potatoes are short, stumpy shoots and not long, thin shoots. The reason for this is because when you put the seed potatoes in the ground, the long, thin shoots will break off very easily, your crop will be okay, but not brilliant.

WHAT TO GROW YOUR POTATOES IN

Now I know that some people think that growing potatoes is a bit of a waste of time, because you can buy them so cheaply in the shops, but let me tell you, once you've tasted a freshly harvested potato for dinner, you will be converted. The flavour is far superior to anything you can buy in the shops, and, if you're starting out, they are one of the easiest vegetables to grow.

There are various ways to grow potatoes. So I'll go through a variety of ways for you to see which ones will suit you best.

Potato grow bags

These are great if you have very limited space, but they can be expensive. Make sure that there are lots of drainage holes in the bottom of the bag, otherwise the water can't escape and you'll end up with a soggy mess. You then need to make sure that you have enough compost to fill the grow bags. Potato grow bags and compost are measured in litres, so you can easily work out how much compost you'll need. You'll also need to sprinkle into the compost some potato fertiliser.

Once you have filled your potato grow bags with compost they'll be very heavy and difficult to move, so I suggest that you decide before you start filling your bags where they're going to go and fill them in situ.

Bags are great for first early and second early potatoes because the potatoes are harvested when they are smaller. But, for main crop potatoes, bags are no good because they'll restrict the growth of your potatoes.

When harvesting your potatoes, bags are very easy, but I will explain more about this a little later.

If the bags are poorly made they will split, so make sure you get good ones.

Buckets

Buckets are a great way to grow your potatoes. They are very sturdy (much more so than bags) and, if you can find buckets with handles, then it makes moving the buckets much easier.

Buckets are expensive though, so it's quite a lot to spend in one go, but they'll last you for years so are a good investment. Make sure you also have plenty of drainage holes in the bottom of each bucket.

The easiest way to make drainage holes in a bucket is by using the largest drill bit you have for your electric drill.

If you are using buckets, they're best for either first early or second early potatoes, but they will restrict the growth of main crop potatoes.

Remember, you will also need to buy enough compost to fill all your buckets to the top, so think about this cost as well. And don't forget to sprinkle in some potato fertiliser.

The Open Ground

This is free, which is always a really great thing, but you'll need to dig over the area that you're going to plant your seed potatoes in very well, and then add some rotted manure and sprinkle on some potato fertiliser. Make sure you gently fork these two extra ingredients into the soil beforehand.

I tend to find that the open ground is no good for first early or second early potatoes because the potatoes are much smaller. When you then come to harvest your potatoes they are sometimes very difficult to see and it's very easy to miss the small ones. Main crop potatoes are perfect for the open ground, it gives them plenty of room in which to spread their roots and grow their crop.

WHAT SOIL DO THEY LIKE?

Potatoes aren't fussy, which is why they grow so well in the UK.

If you are breaking in new soil, then potatoes are the perfect crop to grow because they help to open up the soil.

If you have **clay** soil, adding lots of rotted horse manure to the soil and growing potatoes will help break up the clumps.

Potatoes will also grow very happily in **silty** or **sandy** soils, but also add well rotted horse manure as this will help the fine grains cling together and the manure will absorb water helping the potatoes to grow.

Potatoes can also grow in **chalky** soil, and this will also benefit greatly from horse manure being mixed in with it as it will allow water to be absorbed more easily by the plants.

If you're lucky to have **loamy** soil then you have hit the jackpot. But also add some rotted manure to this soil as well, because it will enrich the soil and the growing potatoes will love it.

What ever soil you have you must also scatter over the soil some potato fertiliser. Potato fertiliser will slowly release nutrients into the soil and help with the growth of your potatoes.

Potato fertiliser is usually found online or in garden centres, but sometimes you're able to get a free packet from Mr Fothergill's when you order your seed potatoes. Wherever you get it from, the instructions on how much to use will be on the packet.

WHEN AND HOW TO PLANT YOUR SEED POTATOES

The times that I'm mentioning below are guidelines only for the south of the UK. It depends where you live, so if you're in a cooler or hotter climate then you will need to adjust slightly.

Extra Early potatoes

Start sowing these in **early March.** Remember these are best sown under cover, because it will still be rather chilly outside. They are best grown in containers and in a greenhouse. As the days get warmer, you can move the containers outside, but be aware that the containers will be rather heavy. You could plant them in a raised bed outside, and then build a mini greenhouse to go over the top, but that is a rather fiddly thing to do. **They must be planted by the end of March at the latest.**

First of all, make sure your container has drainage holes. Then fill your container nearly to the top with a mixture of well rotted manure and multi purpose compost. You can also add some potato fertiliser to the mix as well, but check on the packet as to how much you need to use.

Once the container is full, then take one or two seed potatoes and push them down into the soil about 6 inches and then cover the seed potatoes over with soil.

If you are sowing one seed potato per container then place the seed potato in the centre, if you are sowing two, then place them apart from each other so they have room to spread. Water well.

First Early potatoes

Start sowing your first early potatoes around **late March.** These can be grown either in containers or straight in the open ground. I do tend to find that they are easier to harvest in containers, because some of them can be small and are easily missed in the open soil.

They must be planted by **mid April** at the latest. Again like the extra early potatoes, if you are growing these in a container fill the container to the top with a mixture of manure, multi purpose compost and potato fertiliser. You can plant either one or two seed potatoes per container.

Just like the extra early potatoes, push the seed potatoes down into the compost about 6 inches, and then cover over the seed potato with soil and water well.

Second Early potatoes

Start sowing your second early potatoes from **mid March to mid April.** Again these can either be planted in containers or go straight out in the open ground. Like the first early potatoes they are much easier to harvest from containers, but because they are slightly larger they are fairly easy to harvest in the open ground.

You may miss some of the really small ones, but then we all miss some. They must be planted by the **end of April** at the latest. If you do decide to plant in them in containers just make sure you fill the container to the top with a mixture of manure, multi purpose compost and potato fertiliser.

Sow the seed potatoes 6 inches deep and I would suggest that you only sow one seed potato per container, because these will grow larger and will need more room to grow. If you are planting your second early potatoes in the open ground, the seed potatoes will need to be planted about 12 inches apart and space the rows about 18 inches apart. If you are limited on space then they can be placed a little closer together.

Main crop potatoes

Again these should be planted from **mid March to late April.** These are best grown in the open ground as they need loads of room in which to spread. If you have to grow them in containers, then they may not grow to their maximum size unless you have really large pots. Main crop potatoes are perfect for jacket potatoes, and we all like a good sized jacket spud! These must be planted by the **middle of May** at the latest.

When planting these out in the open soil they need to be planted at least 6 inches deep and about 12-15 inches apart from each other, with rows about 18 inches apart. If you are limited for space, then they can be sown a little closer together.

TO DIG A TRENCH OR NOT DIG A TRENCH?

That is the question. The traditional way to plant your potatoes in the open soil is to dig a trench. My mum did it this way, and so did her dad. It's been done this way for years. The trench can be as long as you need it and at least 6 inches deep. Once you've dug your trench, you line the base of the trench with grass cuttings, vegetable peelings, banana skins, apple cores, or even finely shredded paper. All this gives off nutrients to the growing seed potato and helps retain moisture.

Be aware that if you do dig a trench, that you cover the trench up with plastic over night, otherwise the foxes will mess it up while you sleep.

Digging a trench does take time, and all that digging can make your back hurt a bit, so I don't dig a trench any more. **This is what I do, and it still works perfectly every time:**

Dig over the soil very well, this will allow oxygen to get into the soil. Then I'll add a good amount of horse manure and some potato fertiliser and gently fork that in as well. Then rake over the bed to make sure that it's level.

I then get my seed potatoes and place them on the surface of the soil. I'll place mine about 12-15 inches apart and then leave a gap between rows of about 15-18 inches.

I have a wonderful tool from Joseph Bentley and it's a long handled bulb planter. I don't use it for planting bulbs, but for planting my seed potatoes. It's perfect! If you want to get one, then make sure that you get this one, you'll find it on their website for about £35. There are some cheaper ones out there, but the cheap ones don't last. I know I've tried them. I've now had the same planter for about 5 years and it's still going strong.

To plant your seed potatoes:

Lift up one seed potato, push the bulb planter in to the soil as far as you can to make a hole, then, as you pull the planter out of the soil, it leaves a hole. Pop one seed potato in each hole.

Then continue down your line to the next potato and so on until you've finished. You'll find that you get your seed potatoes planted in no time at all and it's very easy.

Once all you seed potatoes are planted, then just rake over the soil to fill in the holes, job done!

Then, just so you remember where the rows are, insert a bamboo cane into the soil and a label with the variety of potato written on it.

WHAT TO EXPECT AS THEY GROW

Once you have sown your seed potatoes you'll see nothing happening for about 3-4 weeks. But don't worry, because under the ground they're working away very hard.

Your seed potatoes will be sending out roots down into the soil and the shoots will be working their way up through the soil to reach the sunshine.

The roots take in water and other nutrients to help the plant grow. You don't need to water your plants at this stage, usually we have plenty of rain in the Spring, but if you do live in a very dry climate then water your seed potatoes very well once a week.

After about 3-4 weeks you'll see some shoots and leaves appear out of the soil. Make sure that as soon as they appear you immediately cover them over with more soil. You need to keep the leaves covered at this early stage because if you get a frost, then the frost will kill the leaves and the potato plant either won't grow, or will grow very small.

Once all frost has gone in your area then you don't need to worry about covering them up any more. If you have a light frost late in the spring, then don't worry as the plant is usually big enough to cope.

Frost dates for your area can be found very easily on the internet. This is a great site to use http://www.gardenaction.co.uk/main/weather.asp

---

Once the plants start to appear above the ground, then water very well once a week. If you live in a hot climate you may have to water twice a week. The best way to water is to either use a hose or a watering can, so the water goes directly down into the soil and straight to the seed potato.

Above the soil your plants should get to about 2-3 feet tall and the leaves and stems should be a wonderful green colour.

FEEDING YOUR POTATOES AS THEY GROW

Before you planted your seed potatoes in the soil, you had already added some potato fertiliser and some manure to the soil. But potatoes are very hungry plants so as they grow they'll need some extra food to keep them going.

I'm a firm believer in Shropshire Seaweed Fertiliser. This can be bought online and I've now been using it for several years and have harvested the most amazing produce. It can be used to feed all sorts of plants.

The largest potato I ever harvested was a main crop Sarpo Mira and weighed just under 2lb! It did mashed potato for 5 adults. The instructions are on the bottle and it will tell you how much you need to use, but it's worth every penny, so I would recommend you use this. Also as the potatoes grow, if you have any spare well rotted horse manure, just spread it round the base of each plant, this will feed them and make them grow beautifully.

WILL MY POTATOES GET FLOWERS AND SMALL GREEN FRUITS?

As your potato plants grow, you will notice that most varieties of potatoes produce little flowers, which will then turn into little green fruits, which look like little green tomatoes. Please don't eat these little fruits as they don't taste good.

The potato plants produce these at the end of their growing season and if you're growing extra early, first early or second early potatoes, then this is a sign that your potatoes are ready to harvest.

If you are growing main crop potatoes then they are not ready yet. For main crop potatoes you have to wait until the stems and leaves of the plant have lost their green colour and have gone yellow or brown. If there is still green colour in the stem and leaves, then there is still goodness in the plant to help the potatoes grow bigger.

HOW TO HARVEST

Let's start with the **extra early** potatoes first.

They are ready to harvest when the flowers have turned into fruits. Remember, this variety of potato is best grown in a container, so they are very easy to harvest. Cut off the stems of the plants about 3 inches above the soil.

Then place a large piece of plastic sheeting on the ground and gently tip the entire contents of the container out onto the plastic sheet.

Do one plant at a time to make sure they are ready to harvest. If some of the potatoes are a little too small or still green, then leave the other plants for another couple of weeks and then harvest.

Once you've emptied the contents of one container onto the plastic sheeting, all you need to do is to rummage around in the compost and harvest all the potatoes you find. Because they're in a container there is no chance of missing any.

Once you have harvested all your potatoes, then place the spent compost either on your allotment, or garden, or on the compost heap.

Please don't place the compost back in the container to use again for more potatoes the following year as this may spread some viruses.

Harvesting first early and second early potatoes

For first early and second early potatoes, again if you are growing them in pots, cut off the stems and then check each container one at a time to make sure the potatoes are ready and none of them are green.

If you do find that the potatoes are not quite big enough yet, and some potatoes are still green, then place the entire plant back in the container for another couple of weeks. The longer your potatoes are in the compost the larger they'll become, but you can't eat green potatoes as they're poisonous.

Potatoes usually go green due to exposure to the light, it's all to do with the formation of chlorophyll which produces toxins in the potato which are harmful to humans. That is why some of your potatoes that grow near the surface of the soil may be green. Small amounts of the toxins are ok, but too much causes a very bad upset stomach. If your potatoes are really green they will also taste bitter. If you have a slightly green potato, peel the green section and if it's just skin deep then the potato is fine, but if the inside of the potato is green as well then discard it.

The tops of the potato plants can be put directly in the compost heap and then they'll break down and make wonderful compost to feed your plants the following year, **but remember not to reuse the**

compost the following year for more potatoes as they may spread viruses.

If you are growing your first early and second early potatoes in the open ground, then it's best to use a large fork to harvest them. Place the prongs of the fork about 6 inches away from the base of plants, and push the fork into the ground as far as it'll go.

Pull the fork back, and hopefully your potatoes will rise to the surface of the soil. Move the fork all the way round the base of the plant and soon you'll be able to lift out your potato plant.

As you pull the plant out of the soil then some of the potatoes will still be attached, so they're easy to harvest. To retrieve the other potatoes, you'll have to get down on your hands and knees and move the soil to try and find the rest. This can sometimes take quite a while and using a trowel to scrape away the soil is very helpful.

It is very easy to miss small potatoes if grown in the open ground, so make sure that you dig thoroughly so as not to miss any.

Don't harvest your potatoes using a large spade, because you'll end up slicing through the potatoes.

If you use a fork, then you'll just get a prong through a few of them.

Harvesting main crop potatoes.

These are best grown in open ground because they need more room to grow.

Harvest your main crop potatoes when the leaves and stems of the potato plants have turned yellow. Once the green colour has gone from the plant, then the potatoes under the ground won't grow anymore.

To harvest these from the soil you'll need a large garden fork.

Plunge the prongs of the fork into the soil about 9 inches from the base of the potato plant and push down into the soil as far as it'll go.

Pull the fork back to open up the soil and then dig around the plant to make it easier to lift the plant out. Once you've opened up the soil, grab the stems and gently pull up. Using your fork, dig the soil and lift up the soil to help bring up your potatoes. Main crop potatoes can spread quite a way, so make sure that you dig very throughly.

Again it's best to use a fork rather than a spade because it's very easy to cut a potato in half using a spade.

Discard the stems of the plants in the compost heap.

PESTS AND DISEASES

When growing potatoes, usually they'll grow without incident. If you are growing potatoes in the open soil, then it is best to grow in a different place each year, as this will stop the spread of any pests and diseases. If growing in containers, always clean the containers thoroughly each year and fill with new compost. Again this will stop the spread of any pests and diseases.

Even with all these precautions there are still some pests and diseases that you must look out for.

Blight

Blight affects the entire potato plant and you can lose your entire crop. The signs to look out for first are on the leaves and stem. This usually happens in August, if the weather is very humid and wet. You will see brown patches appear on the leaves. On the underside of the leaves you will find white mouldy patches. As soon as you see any evidence of blight on the leaves then cut off all the stems to about two inches above the soil.

Do not under any circumstances put the diseased leaves on your compost heap as they will spread the disease and infect the soil.

The leaves and stems must be either burnt, or taken to your recycling centre. The potatoes can be left in the soil for a few weeks more, but dig up one plant and, if the potatoes are ready (none are green), then harvest them all. If you leave the leaves on, then the disease will work its way very quickly down to the potatoes and you'll then find strange markings, either reddish brown or grey patches on the skins of the potatoes. The potatoes will then go soft and rot in storage.

There is no cure for blight, but since I've been growing Sarpo Mira potatoes, which are blight resistant, from Mr Fothergill's Seeds I've never had a problem with blight.

Leaf roll virus

You may notice that the green leaves start to turn in and roll up, this is call leaf roll virus.

You'll find that if you get this, then your plants will only grow to be very small, and the potatoes under the soil will be few and far between.

Unfortunately there is no treatment to cure this, but the affected plant can be sprayed to slow down the spread of it.

I've had this a few times, but it doesn't seem to spread to any of the other surrounding plants. Maybe I've just been lucky. You don't need to remove the leaves, but once you harvest the potatoes don't put the leaves and stem on the compost heap.

Slugs

Yes, they eat potatoes as well. Slugs are a real pain because they seem to eat anything that you plant. They're an absolute nightmare for all gardeners.

When you harvest your potatoes, you may find some small holes on the outside of the potatoes and when you then cut into the potatoes you will see holes which look like tunnels all the way through the entire potato, slugs have made these. Slugs are usually a big problem if you are growing your potatoes in clay soil. So, before you plant your seed potatoes in clay soil, try to dig in as much rotted horse manure as you can. This will break up the clods of clay and the slugs will venture elsewhere.

Common scab

You may also find that when you harvest your potatoes, they have brown scabby patches dotted on their skins. This is called common scab. It sounds awful, but please don't worry about it. The scab is only on the skin of the potato but the rest of the potato is absolutely fine and can be eaten. Just peel the potato to get rid of the scab. Scab happens when you plant your potatoes in light soils and they don't get enough water.

To avoid most of these diseases, make sure that you get your seed potatoes from a trusted source. The big seed companies have very good produce for you to buy.

Also, make sure that every seed potato you plant is healthy right from the start. If they have any mouldy patches or are soft even before you plant them, then they won't grow well. So before you plant them in the soil give them a good inspection and get rid of any sub-standard ones.

Also make sure that you water and feed your potatoes regularly. They are thirsty and hungry plants so will need enough water and food to make them grow to their maximum potential.

There are plenty of other pests and diseases that you may get while growing your potatoes, but I've just highlighted the most common ones.

HOW TO STORE POTATOES

Once you've harvested all your wonderful potatoes they'll last for ages if they are stored properly. One year, I grew so many potatoes that my harvest kept our family going for an entire year.

You can only store perfect potatoes, so any with defects must be eaten as soon as possible and not stored.

The reason for this is because a defect in a potato could go mouldy and then ruin the other potatoes that are near it. Before you know it, loads of your potatoes would have gone mouldy and you could lose the lot.

Before you store your potatoes, you must make sure that you sort through each and every potato carefully. Brush most of the dirt off them, do not wash them because this will get them damp and mould spores could grow.

Once you have brushed off the dirt, then the best way to store them is to use a fabric sack, I bought mine from Mr Fothergill's Seeds. Fabric sacks allow the potatoes to breathe and air can circulate.

Fabric sacks are very large, so do not overfill the sack to the top as you will stop the air from circulating, and also you won't be able to move the full sack.

You can also get small fabric bags which are good. Leave the top of the bag open to let the air circulate.

Large plastic stackable trays are good (like the ones bread gets delivered in), because they have holes in them and again the air can circulate round the potatoes. Although not many of us have access to these.

Under no circumstances should you store your potatoes in plastic bags. The potatoes will sweat and go mouldy.

Once your potatoes are in their bag, sack or tray, then they must be stored in a dark frost-free place. A garage is ideal, or a shed. I store mine in a wooden shed.

Do not store them in the greenhouse as the potatoes will start to go green because of the sunlight and then they'll start to send out sprouts.

Even if you are storing your potatoes in the dark, you will eventually find that your potatoes do start to send out shoots. Don't worry about this. You can still eat the potatoes, just pick off the sprout.

HOW TO COOK YOUR POTATOES

Potatoes can be roasted, mashed, fried, boiled, sautéed - they're so versatile!

But, what do you do with the really small ones that you harvest? Some people just throw them away, but not me. When I come across some really small potatoes, I give them a good clean, I don't peel them, because that's just silly, and I put them in a casserole. That way you don't have to use an extra pan to make mashed potatoes and the entire meal is cooked in one dish. Less washing up as well, which is always a good thing.

Freshly harvested potatoes taste amazing, there is nothing like it. They're so fresh and flavourful. Boil some new potatoes with some fresh mint and then, once they're cooked, add a knob of butter and sprinkle over some fresh chives.

Or cut your potatoes into 1 inch cubes, add a little salt, pepper and olive oil and roast for about 45 minutes in a medium oven. Makes a wonderful change to chips for dinner. You can always add some spices to the potatoes to give them a more exotic flavour.

Go on and give them a try, you won't be disappointed.

POTATO RECIPE

There are many ways to cook your potatoes, but if you fancy trying something a little different then why not give this potato rosti recipe a go.

Ingredients

- 1 small red onion
- 2 large potatoes
- Salt and pepper
- A small knob of butter
- A little olive oil

Method

1. Peel and cut a red onion very finely, and place on a clean tea towel.
2. Wash and dry the potatoes, but leave the skins on.

3. Using the coarse side of a metal box grater, grate the potatoes and place on the tea towel with the onions.
4. Gather the tea towel up to make a ball and squeeze as much liquid out the potatoes and onions as you can.
5. Put the squeezed potatoes and onions in a bowl and add some salt and pepper and mix well.
6. Heat the butter and oil in a large frying pan until it starts to sizzles.
7. Put the onion and potato mix in the frying pan and pat down firmly.
8. Fry for about 5-7 minutes on one side before carefully turning over and fry again for about 5-7 minutes on the other side. Each side should be mid golden brown in colour.
9. Once cooked place on some kitchen towel to remove any excess oil.

PARSNIPS

INTRODUCTION

Parsnips are a root vegetable, which means that their roots swell under the ground. As the plant grows, and when we harvest them, we eat the swollen roots.

They are closely related to carrots, and have a sweet, earthy flavour to them. They can be eaten raw in winter salads, but usually they are cooked. Cooking parsnips brings out their sweet flavour.

Parsnips are biennials, which means that they take 2 years to complete their lifecycle. If you do leave any parsnips in the ground for 2 years, they will produce flowers, and then seeds. The seeds can then be sown in the soil to produce your next harvest of parsnips. But this will make the root of the parsnips very woody and inedible.

Usually parsnips are grown as annuals, so are harvested at the end of their first year, and not allowed to go to seed. If you want to produce your own seeds, then allow one plant to continue growing for 2 years and harvest the rest after the first year.

Parsnips are high in vitamins C and K and also Magnesium, as well as many other vitamins and minerals, so are an excellent addition to our daily diet.

Parsnips have been grown since Greek and Roman times, and were very popular, although they may have been confused with white carrots, which were also very popular during those times.

Parsnips are native to Europe and Asia and, because of their sweet flavour, were used as a form of sweetener before sugar became available.

Parsnips were introduced to North America in the 16th century, and were the main source of starch in meals. But by the mid 19th century, the parsnips popularity started to decline as potatoes were used instead.

There are many ways in which you can cook your parsnips, from roasting, boiling, frying, and even steaming.

Roasted parsnips are an essential part of the English Sunday Roast dinner, but are perfect any day of the week.

WHEN TO SOW PARSNIPS

Parsnips seeds can be sown in February, but the weather can still be very cold. If you do sow your parsnip seeds this early, the germination rate will be very low.

But if you want to sow your parsnip seeds in February, make sure that you cover your seeds with a plastic cloche to help keep in some heat.

A cloche a long plastic tunnel, and they come in various sizes. They are perfect if you need to sow your seeds early as they protect your seeds from the weather. Cloches will help keep in some heat and protect your seedling from the strong winds, rain and cold weather.

Cloches can be bought online, from gardening centres or from gardening catalogues. Cloches come in a variety of sizes, so choose which is best for you.

Before sowing your seeds, warm the soil with the cloche. To warm the soil, all you have to do this put the cloche over the area where you're going to sow your seeds. Do this a couple of weeks before sowing your seeds.

Once you have sown your seeds, keep the cloche over your parsnip seedlings as they grow. Don't take the cloche off until your parsnip seedlings are at least 3 inches tall.

If you can wait until the middle of March to sow your parsnip seeds, then you won't have to use a cloche to protect them, unless that is, you live in a very cold climate. Parsnip seeds can be sown up until May, so don't be in a hurry to get your parsnip seeds in the ground.

Parsnip seeds are very slow to germinate, taking anywhere between 10-28 days. So be patient and sow slightly more than you want. The later you sow your parsnip seeds, the better their germination rate will be.

HOW TO SOW YOUR PARSNIP SEEDS

Always use fresh parsnip seeds every year. Parsnips seeds don't keep for more than one year. If you do have some parsnips seeds from a previous year, you can still sow them, but the germination rate will be much lower.

To grow to their full potential, parsnips need free draining soil, with very few stones in it. As a parsnip grows down into the ground, it will push through the soil to find water. If there are any obstacles in its path it will grow round them. This is why you sometimes get wonky looking parsnips, or parsnips that have several legs.

Parsnip seeds are light brown, circular and flat. Be very careful when sowing them, as the slightest breeze will blow them away.

Parsnips are best sown in rows, as this makes looking after them much easier as they grow.

Before you start to sow your seeds, you must give the soil a good forking over with a large fork. Dig down in the soil as far as you can, and turn the soil over. This helps break up the soil, and allows oxygen to get into the soil. Remove any weeds, break up any large clods of soil, and remove any large stones.

Once you have done all this, rake the soil so it's level.

Next you'll need to make a straight line using some string. The straight line helps you keep your seeds lovely and neat when you come to sow them. It doesn't matter how long your line is.

The best way to make a straight line is by using some string and a couple of metal stakes.

Tie one end of the string to one of the metal stakes, and the other end of the string to the other metal stake. Push one stake into the soil at the beginning of the line you want to make, and the other stake at the other end of the line. Wind the string up around one stake so the string is tight.

Scoop out a shallow trough, about half an inch deep, all along the string line. Remove any large clods of soil, and any stones that you may have missed when digging.

Then, water in the trough you have just made. Fill the trough with water and allow it to soak through the soil. Watering the trough will also level out the soil. Also, when you sow your seeds, they will stick to the damp soil and not blow away.

Because the germination rate for parsnips can be quite low, you'll need to sow more seeds than you need. It's best to sow a group of 3 seeds together, and space the groups of seeds about 5 inches apart. Do this all along the trough.

If you are sowing more than one row of parsnips, make sure your rows are about 9 inches apart from each other. That way you can still get in-between your parsnips to weed, and there is still enough room for your parsnips to spread as they grow.

Once you have sown your seeds you'll need to cover them very carefully with some soil. Once your seeds are covered, gently pat the soil down.

Put a stick at both ends of your line of parsnips, and insert a label at one end. Make sure you write what variety you are growing as well.

You won't need to water your seeds again until the soil feels dry. Don't over water your seeds as they will rot and won't germinate at all. The best way to test if your soil is dry, is by sticking your forefinger into the soil up to your first knuckle. If the soil feels damp it's fine and you won't need to water. If the soil feels dry then you will need to water, but only a little.

The varieties of parsnips I like to grow are either "**Gladiator F1**", which produce wonderful large roots, and have a very smooth and sweet flavour. They are also one of the first varieties of parsnip you can harvest, which can be as early as October.

Also I love to grow a variety called "**Tender and True**", which have a high germination rate. This variety are not as large as some other varieties of parsnips, but they have a wonderful flavour when roasted.

GROWING PARSNIPS IN RAISED BEDS OR CONTAINERS

Because parsnips have a long root, they need to be able to grow down a very long way. Therefore growing in raised beds or containers can be difficult. But it can be done.

You must make sure that your raised beds or containers are at least 2 foot deep and no less 6 inches wide, but they can be as long as you like.

> I know that 2 foot deep sounds a lot, but I've grown parsnips before that were 18 inches long once. And they were a bugger to dig up I can tell you.

Make sure your raised bed or container has plenty of drainage holes in the bottom, and the soil is free draining.

To help with drainage, put some large stones or broken terracotta at the very bottom, then a layer of well rotted manure on top of that. Then fill the remaining space with soil and some sand. Adding in a little sand to the soil also helps with the drainage.

If you want to mix some manure in with the soil, make sure that it is very well broken down, and there are no large lumps in it. If there are, then this will stop the parsnips from growing lovely and straight.

Sow the seeds in the same way as you would in the open ground.

If you are unable to have a raised bed or container at least 2 feet deep, then there is a variety of parsnip called "**Avonresister**" then grow to about 6 inches long, and are perfect for growing in a shallow space. However, these are very difficult to find as most of the major seed companies don't do them. You might be lucky enough to find some online.

THE FIRST LEAVES

Parsnips seeds take between 10-28 days to germinate, so be patient with them. The first leaves that poke through the soil will be the plants two baby leaves, and bear no resemblance to the rest of the plants leaves.

The baby leaves are long, green and narrow.

As the seedling grows, more leaves will appear from between the baby leaves. All the other leaves will be oval and have bumps round the outside of the leaf. As the leaves then grow, the bumps will separate out and make individual leaves.

As your parsnips grow, the baby leaves will slowly shrivel away and drop off. You won't notice this happen, and if the baby leaves go yellow or brown, don't worry.

All the other leaves of the parsnip, will grow from the centre, and they will grow quite tall.

HOW TO LOOK AFTER YOUR PARSNIPS AS THEY GROW

Parsnips are very easy to look after as they grow, and don't need a huge amount of attention. But there are a few things you must do to keep your plants happy, so they can reach their full potential.

Thinning out

You may need to thin out you seedlings as they grow. Because the germination rate of parsnips can be little low, you'll always need to sow more seeds that you need.

I sow my parsnips in groups of 3 seeds. Usually only 1 or 2 seeds from that group will germinate. If you find that more than one seed from each group germinates, you will need to remove any of the extra ones.

Do not thin out your seedlings until they are at least 4 or 5 inches tall.

When thinning out your seedlings, make sure there is enough room in-between each seedling, so your parsnips can swell as they grow. Each parsnip should swell to about 3 inches across. Although some can grow smaller or much larger.

Remove any of the weakest seedlings, and always leave the strongest of the group of seeds to continue to grow.

Because the seedlings are still very tiny, they should be very easy to just pull out with your thumb and finger. You should not disturb the soil when you do this, because the seedlings are only small.

Go along your line of parsnips very carefully, pulling out the seedlings you don't want. When you have finished thinning them out you should give your seedlings a little water. This will make sure that any soil that has been disturbed settles back around the seedlings again.

Weeding

Make sure that you weed around your parsnip seedlings very carefully. Weeds grow much faster than the parsnip seedlings, so if you don't weed regularly, the weeds will take over and will cover your parsnip seedlings and suffocate them. You seedlings will then all die and you won't have any to harvest.

Parsnip seedlings are very delicate, and will damage very easily. The only way to weed at this stage is by getting down on your hands and knees.

When your parsnips are established in the soil then you can use a hoe to control the weeds. If you accidentally break off some of your parsnip's large leaves this won't be a problem, but make sure you don't damage the growing parsnip root. If you damage the root, infection may get in, and then you could lose some of your parsnips to disease.

Watering

Make sure you don't over water your parsnips as they grow. Your growing plants will send down a tap root, deep into the soil. The tap root will search out water in the soil. If you water your parsnips too often, then you'll end up with short, stumpy parsnips, rather than long parsnips.

Once you have sown your seeds, only water when the soil is dry. When your seedlings are tiny, use a fine rose on the end of your watering can spout. When your parsnips are larger and more robust, then you can use a rose with larger holes.

When your parsnips are established and growing well, you should only need to water them every other week.

Even in the height of summer and during a heatwave, you'll only need to water your parsnips once a week.

Feeding

Parsnips are hungry plants, and will need feeding.

There are numerous plant feeds to choose from. You can either get all purpose liquid feeds, pellets, granules, or powders. The best thing to do is to go to your local garden centre, and choose which ever one suits you best. They are all very good, but follow the directions they give you. They vary quite a lot in price, so whatever fits in with your budget.

We all have our favourite feed, and mine is **Shropshire Seaweed Fertiliser**. I've been using this for several years now, and I find that it makes all my plants grow beautifully every year. It's only available online and not available in the shops.

PESTS AND DISEASES

There are only a few problems that you may have when growing parsnips. One is **parsnip canker**, another is **carrot fly**, and the last one is **fanging or forking.**

Let me give you a little more information on these and how to avoid them.

Parsnip canker

You will know if your parsnips have canker, because you will notice the skin of your parsnip turning either orange, brown or black, and it'll become very rough like a horrible scab.

It usually starts at the top of the parsnip and then works its way down to the end of the root.

Sometimes the canker scabs are large and cover the entire parsnip root, but other times there will be small blotches all the way down the root.

Canker is a fungal disease, and can stay in the soil for several years. The best way to try and control canker is to grow a resistant variety. "**Gladiator F1**", "**Countess F1**" or "**Duchess F1**" are very good. Although most varieties are now canker resistant.

Also make sure that you grow your parsnips in a different place each year, as this will stop the disease from spreading.

Growing your parsnips in free draining soil also helps. If you have clay soil, try mixing in some well rotted manure, and adding some sand into the soil as well should help.

Parsnip like to grow in lime soil, so before you sow your seeds, and if your soil is very acidic, sprinkle on a little lime to help change the PH of you soil.

Lime can be bought very easily in garden centres and DIY stores. Always read the instructions on the back of the box as it'll give you instructions on how much to use.

However, if your parsnips do get canker, then there is no cure. You should harvest your parsnips immediately and then store them in boxes of damp sand. Check your parsnips weekly for any damage. If you do find any evidence of canker on your stored parsnips, use them up immediately. You can still cook and eat them, but make sure you cut out any damaged parts of the parsnip first.

Make sure you clear away any parsnip leaves from the soil, dig the soil very throughly and leave over winter.

Carrot fly

Yes parsnips can get carrot fly. I know it seems odd, but both carrots and parsnips are root vegetables, and are closely related.

Be very careful when weeding and thinning out your parsnips, because if you damaged any of your growing parsnips, they will release a smell that attracts the carrot fly.

The carrot fly will then land on your parsnips, lay its eggs in your parsnips, and, when the eggs hatch, the babies nibble their way through your parsnips.

If your parsnips get carrot fly, then you'll notice black lines through your parsnips.

There is no cure for carrot fly, so prevention is the best cure.

Make sure the air can circulate freely around your parsnips, and when you thin your seedlings out, or weed around them, be very careful to not damage the roots of the parsnips.

Once you have finished thinning or weeding your parsnips, water them and the soil around directly around them, as the water will suppress the smell of the parsnips.

You can still eat parsnips that have got carrot fly, just cut out the damaged part of the parsnip.

If you are planting your parsnips seeds in February, cover them with a cloche, as this will protect them. If you are sowing your seeds later, from mid March, then you shouldn't need to cover them with a cloche, but you can if you want to.

Fanging or forking

This is when your parsnips root splits into two or more, and you end up with a very odd shaped vegetable. To be honest, I don't mind odd shaped veggies, they have a wonderful charm to them. But if you're exhibiting your crop and want perfectly straight parsnip, this is going to be a no no.

Fanging or forking happens when the root is growing down into the soil, and comes across something solid. This could be a stone, a clod of soil, a tree root, or large lump of manure.

To stop your parsnips ending up with several legs and looking a little like an alien from outer space, you need to make sure you prepare the soil before sowing your seeds.

Dig the soil very well, digging down at least 12-15 inches, breaking down any clods of soil. Remove any large or medium sized stones, and any other debris that you find. Only add manure to the soil the previous autumn, and over the winter it will break down. Dig the manure into the soil a couple of weeks before you plan on sowing your parsnip seeds, and remove any large lumps of manure that have not broken down.

Once you have done all this, level the soil with a rake. Leave the soil to settle for a couple of weeks before sowing your seeds.

WHEN TO HARVEST YOUR PARSNIPS

Parsnips have a very long growing time of about 7 months. If you sow your seeds in March, then you can start harvesting your crop from November and then continue harvesting all the way through to February the following year.

It's always best to wait for a good hard frost in your area before you start to harvest your first parsnips. The frost makes parsnips much sweeter.

Harvest your parsnips as and when you need them. It doesn't matter if you leave your parsnips in the soil throughout the winter months, and they get buried in snow. Parsnips are very hardy plants, and will be fine if the ground freezes. If the ground does freeze, it'll just be a little harder to dig them up.

As the cold weather comes along, you'll find that the leaves on the top of your parsnips die back. Don't worry about this, it's quite normal. The leaves will then start to grow again in February.

This is why it's very important to label where you sow you parsnips, otherwise once the leaves die back, you may forget where they're growing. I forgot where I'd planted some once, and had to wait until the leaves started to grow back to find them.

HOW TO HARVEST YOUR PARSNIPS

When harvesting your parsnips, sometimes you have to use a bit of brute force. If the roots go down a long way, you'll have to do lots of digging.

When digging up your parsnips do not use a spade. If you do, you may slice straight through your parsnip root, and then only be able to pull some of it out of the ground. The best tool to use is a large garden fork.

Position the prongs of the fork at least 3 inches away from the top of the parsnip on one side, and push the fork down into the soil as far as you can.

Pull the fork back, so you start to open up the soil. If the parsnip is still stuck firmly in the soil, then pull the fork out of the soil and repeat the same process on the other side of the parsnip.

When you have opened up the soil as much as you can, grab the top part of the parsnip root firmly with your hand, and give it a wiggle and a gentle pull.

Your parsnip may come up easily, but it may need a little more help.

If your parsnip still doesn't want to come out of the soil then you're going to have to use your fork again to try and dig down even further. Keep pushing your fork into the soil, pulling the fork back to open up the soil. Eventually, and with a lot of perseverance and flexing of your muscles, you will be able to harvest your parsnips.

Once you have harvested as many parsnips as you need, level off the soil again.

Make sure that you harvest all your remaining parsnips by February, otherwise they'll go to seed and the roots will get woody and become inedible.

HOW TO STORE YOUR PARSNIPS

Parsnips can stay in the soil, and you can harvest them as and when you need them. But if your soil gets frozen solid during the winter, then you can harvest your entire crop in November, and store them in a cold garage or shed over the winter.

Only store perfect parsnips. Any with damage to them must be eaten and not stored.

The best way to store your parsnips is to get a large wooden crate and place a thick layer of sand in the bottom. Then lay a single layer of parsnips on the sand, making sure none of your parsnips touch each other.

Cover the parsnips with another thick layer of sand, and then lay some more parsnips on top. Repeat the process until you have filled your box.

The top layer of parsnips must be covered with sand.

Do not use a plastic crate as this will cause the parsnips to sweat and go mouldy. A cardboard crate will get very damp and could go mouldy, which in turn will cause your parsnips to do the same.

If stored correctly, your parsnips should be fine all through the winter.

FREEZING YOUR PARSNIPS

If you are unable to store your parsnips in wooden crates, then you can always freeze them.

Only freeze undamaged parsnips. Any with blemishes on them you'll have to eat first.

Before you freeze your parsnips, you need to make sure you firstly wash them. Then remove any leaves, and cut off the straggly end part of the root.

Next, peel your parsnips, and cut them long ways into even sized pieces. I like my roasted parsnips chunky, so I tend to cut a medium sized parsnip in about 6 pieces. But if you like your roasted parsnips larger or smaller, then cut them to the size you prefer.

Once you have cut your parsnips, place them in a single layer on a baking tray lined with parchment paper. Make sure none of your parsnips are touching each other, and then place the tray of parsnips in the freezer.

This is called "open freezing". This allows each parsnip to freeze individually so it won't get stuck to any other parsnips.

Leave to freeze for 24 hours, and then transfer the frozen parsnips to a plastic freezer bag and place back in the freezer.

Because your parsnips have been frozen individually they won't stick together in the plastic bag.

When you want some parsnips for dinner, all you need to do is to remove what you need from the freezer bag, and put your parsnips in boiling water for 5 minutes. Drain and then roast.

Frozen vegetables will keep perfectly well in the freezer for up to 1 year.

RECIPE - ROASTED PARSNIPS WITH PARMESAN CHEESE

Ingredients

- Parsnips
- Olive oil
- Salt and pepper
- 2 tablespoons of semolina
- 2-3 tablespoons of parmesan cheese

Method

1. Set the oven to Gas 5, 190C, 375F
2. Put a little olive oil on a large baking tray and place on a shelf in the top half of your oven.
3. Clean, peel and cut your parsnips into long lengths. I like chunky parsnips, so I usually cut an average sized parsnip into six pieces.
4. Do not remove the core of the parsnips. I know some

people do, because they think it's woody, but if you grow new parsnips every year you won't get a woody core.

5. Fill a large saucepan two thirds full with cold water, and add a large pinch of salt to the water.
6. Bring the salt water to the boil.
7. When the water is boiling add in your parsnips. Bring the water back up to the boil, and boil your parsnips for just 5 minutes.
8. Drain your parsnip and put in a clean boil.
9. Sprinkle onto your parsnips the semolina and parmesan. As well as a good sprinkling of salt and pepper.
10. Mix them together in the bowl, making sure all the parsnips are coated in the semolina, parmesan, and salt and pepper.
11. Remove the oiled tray from the oven. Be very careful because the soil will be very hot.
12. Put the parsnips on the tray, spreading them out and in one layer.
13. Put the tray of parsnips back in the oven for a bout 30-40 minutes. Turning once during the cooking time.
14. Your parsnips will be ready when the ends of your parsnips start to crisp up and turn a dark brown, and the middle of the parsnips are just turning golden brown.

They are the perfect accompaniment to any roast dinner. Fewer and fewer people are growing parsnips these days, because they take a long time to grow, but parsnips are so delicious.

So come on, let the parsnip revival start here.

RADISHES

TYPES OF RADISH

We all think of radishes as a summer vegetable, because most of us grow them during the summer months. But there are two varieties of radish: winter and summer.

Winter radish

There are only a few varieties of winter radish, so you may have to hunt around for these. They need to be sown from May through to the end of August. These you'll be harvesting throughout the winter. The roots of the winter radishes are much larger and longer than the summer varieties, and also have a much stronger flavour. The skins of the winter varieties are also thicker, and the skins of the roots will look a lot rougher than their summer counterparts.

I would recommend you try "China Rose", which is a long, oval, red radish. They look a bit knobbly, but it has a fresh crisp flavour. Or if you wanted to try something a little different why not try "Black

Spanish Round". They're exactly as the name says, round, with black skins. The inside of the radish is white and they're very tasty.

You should start to harvest your winter radishes from September through to December.

Summer radish

The summer varieties of radishes have very thin skins, and are either round or oval in shape, but you can find a few varieties that are long and thin.

Summer radish can be sown from the middle of March through to the middle of June. You will be harvesting your summer radish from middle of June through to the middle of August.

Most seed companies have a very good selection of summer radish, and there are plenty to choose from.

When I grow radishes I like to make sure they look interesting and are very colourful, so every year I always sow "Bright Lights". They come in an array of yellow, pink, red, purple, white and duel coloured radish. They are round and are incredibly tasty. If you want your radish to all to be the same colour, then I would suggest "Esmeralda F1". These radish are oval, with the very bottom of the radish white, but the top of the radish a bright pink colour. They are full of flavour and can be sown all year round, but during the winter months they must be protected by a cloche or cover.

WHEN TO SOW YOUR RADISH SEEDS

Radishes can be sown successionally throughout the growing season. Successionally means you can sow some seeds every couple of weeks throughout the growing season. That way, you'll get a continuous supply of radishes all summer or winter long.

Once radishes are ready they need to be harvested immediately. If they are left in the ground and go past their best, they will go hard and woody inside, and you won't be able to eat them.

From sowing to harvesting, your radishes don't take very long. Summer varieties you'll be harvesting in just 3-6 weeks, whereas winter varieties you'll be harvesting in 10-12 weeks.

Summer varieties should be sown directly outside in the soil from the middle of March through to the beginning of June.

Winter varieties, should also be sown directly in the soil, and can be sown from the middle of May through to the end of August.

You can start your Summer radishes off at the beginning of

February, but they must be grown undercover or in an unheated greenhouse. They make take a little longer to grow because the climate is cooler, but only a couple of weeks or so.

Radishes are very hardy plants, and are best sown directly outside in the soil. There is no need to start them off early in small pots or cells.

Summer radish like the sun, but if the weather is too hot during the summer months, then their roots won't swell up and all you'll end up with are long thin spindly roots.

When you sow your radish seeds in March and April, they can be sown in full sun, but when you come to sow them in May and June, it's best to sow them under a little bit of shade.

Because winter radish are sown in the summer months, they are best sown in partial shade.

PREPARING THE SOIL

Radishes prefer to grow in well drained soil. Make sure you have also incorporated plenty of organic matter in the soil as well. Well rotted horse manure, chicken manure pellets or anything well rotted from the bottom of your compost heap is perfect.

Make sure the soil has been dug over throughly, and you have removed any weeds and large stones. It is very important that you remove any large stones and break down any large clods of earth, especially if you are growing long radishes. If a long radish comes in contact with an obstacle, then the root will split and you'll end up with a very odd shaped radish.

Once you have dug over the soil, then add in your organic matter and fork in lightly, make sure you then level the soil over with a rake, and leave it to settle for a day before sowing your seeds.

HOW TO SOW YOUR RADISH SEEDS

Sowing radishes is very easy to do, all you need is some string attached to a metal pole either end (so you can make sure you get a straight line), a trowel, watering can, a label, a couple of small sticks and of course your choice of radish seeds.

Using the string and poles mark out a straight line. Make sure you don't make the line too long, because you don't want to be overrun with radishes when they are ready to harvest. I find that a line of about 2 feet long is perfect.

Remember you'll be sowing more seeds every couple of weeks, so you don't want to sow too many each time.

Using your trowel, scoop out the soil along your string line, making a long trough about half an inch deep.

Using a watering can, without the rose attachment, water the trough and allow the water to drain right through into the soil. Watering before you sow your seeds, helps to level off the soil in the trough and when you sow the seeds, they are immediately in contact with some water, so will start to germinate.

Next you need to sow your radish seeds. Tip some into the palm of one hand, and using your thumb and forefinger, from your other hand, take a pinch of seeds and sprinkle them into the trough.

Move your finger and thumb back and forth so the radish seeds distribute evenly. Radish roots need to swell, so make sure you leave about 1 inch between each seed. If some are a little closer together, or further apart, don't worry.

Once you have sown your seeds cover them over with some more soil, and give the soil a gentle pat down. Put a label at one end of the line, and a small stick at the other, then you know where the line of radish begin and end.

You won't need to water for a couple of days, and when you do water make sure you put the rose attachment on the end of the watering can spout.

The germination rate for radishes is very good, so make sure you don't overcrowd them.

GROWING RADISH IN RAISED BEDS OR CONTAINERS

Radishes are perfect for growing in raised beds or containers. Most radishes are either round or oval, so therefore don't need much depth to grow.

If you are growing radishes in a container you must make sure the container is at least 6 inches deep. This will allow the radish root to grow downwards and allow it to search for water. If you are growing the long radish "Mooli" or "Candela di fuoco" for example, then these will need a depth of about 15 inches in which to grow properly.

Whatever varieties of radish you grow in a raised bed or container, they need to be sown in exactly the same way as you would in the open ground.

THE FIRST LEAVES

After about 7-10 days your radishes will start to germinate, and you'll see the first leaves appear.

Sometimes the first leaves are called baby leaves. Two leaves will grow, and these leaves looked like a squashed heart shape. As your radish plants grow more leaves will grow, but they will look completely different to the baby leaves. The rest of the other leaves will be on long stems, and sort-of oval in shape.

You'll also notice that the leaves will be slightly prickly. These prickles will not be large and sharp and pointy, but just make the leaves rough to the touch.

HOW TO LOOK AFTER YOUR RADISHES AS THEY GROW

Radishes are a very easy crop to look after as they don't suffer from many problems. But there are a few things you can do to help them grow really well.

Watering

Radishes need regular watering to help them grow, so their roots can swell. Water thoroughly when you sow them, and then twice a week. If you have a heavy downpour of rain a day before you are due to water, then you won't need to water your radishes.

When the seedlings are small, make sure you only use a fine rose on the end of your watering can spout. Once your radish plants get established, then you can use a rose with slightly larger holes.

If you sow some radish during the summer months, you may have to water 3 times a week. Summer radishes prefer a cooler temperature, and seem to do much better when sown earlier in the Spring, rather than later. Winter radishes grow better when sown in early Summer.

Weeding

Weeds spread very fast and will suffocate any of your radish seedlings as they try to grow. Make sure you weed around your radish seedlings very carefully every week. Also try not to damage any of the growing plants as this could allow disease to get into the swelling roots. Once you have weeded, water the soil. Watering is essential, as it gently pushes back the soil around the radish plants and fills in any air pockets in the soil.

Feeding

Radishes are hungry plants and will need regular feeding. There are lots of feeds available, so just choose one that is best for you. You can either get an all purpose liquid plant feed, pellets, granules or powders.

Pop along to your local garden centre and see what they have on offer. They are all very good, and vary in price, so choose whatever fits your budget.

I prefer to use Shropshire Seaweed Fertiliser as I have used this for many years and it produces excellent results every time. It is only available online.

Thinning out

Radish roots need room to swell, so make sure you don't grow them too close to one another.

As your seedlings grow, you may notice that some are growing too close to each other, so you'll have to remove some. This is best done when you are weeding. Gently pull up any unwanted seedlings out of the ground. They should come out very easily. Once you have thinned out your seedlings, give the soil a water.

Make sure your radishes are growing approximately 1-2 inches apart from each other. This way they will have plenty of growing space.

If you wish, you could replant any of the seedlings you've removed back into the soil, to make another line of radish. Make sure you plant immediately and then water them in well and they should be fine, however, you may lose a few.

PESTS AND DISEASES

Radishes aren't prone to too many pests and diseases, but there are a few things you need to be aware of.

Birds

Birds can be a problem, especially pigeons. Birds like to eat the fresh green leaves of your radishes, but only the new leaves before they get too big and the prickles on the leaves start to develop.

If birds are a problem for you, then the best way to protect your plants is to place a small, arched tunnel of very fine wire over the top of your plants. This way the birds will be unable to get to the leaves. But the time the leaves start to grow through the wire, they will be too tough for the birds to eat.

Slugs and snails

Slugs and snails can also be a bit of a problem, but there are some easy ways to stop them attacking your plants. They will try and eat the fresh new shoots, and once the leaves get too large they won't touch them, because of the prickles.

Make sure you clear any debris and weeds from around your radish roots, because clear soil is not somewhere a slug or snail wants to be. Keeping the area clear means you won't need to put any protection down to repel the slugs and snails.

Flea beetle

Flea beetle may attack the leaves of your radish plants. You may notice small nibbled holes on the leaves of your radish leaves. If your plants are attacked by flea beetle the roots won't be affected, so you will be able to eat your radishes. The leaves of your plants just won't look very attractive.

> You can prevent flea beetle attacking your plants by covering the seedlings with a very fine fleece.

WHEN TO HARVEST YOUR RADISH

You don't have to wait for radish to ripen, they are ready to harvest when they are very small, or you can wait until they grow slightly bigger.

Harvesting summer radish

Summer radish are best harvested about 3-6 weeks after you sow them. Therefore if you sow some seeds in the middle of March, you could be harvesting them from the middle of April. Obviously it depends what the weather has been like. If the weather has been really cold, then your radish will take a little longer. If you sow some seeds at the beginning of June, you should be harvesting them at the beginning of July.

Harvesting winter radish

Winter radish take longer to grow. From sowing to harvesting takes about 10-12 weeks. With this in mind, if you sow some seeds in the middle of May, you should be harvesting them by the beginning of August. If you sow some late in the season at the end of August, then you might not harvest them until January the following year.

In both cases, if the leaves of your radish suddenly shoot up and flowers start to grow, your radish plant has started to go to seed. If this happens, then the inside of your radish will have gone hard or "woody", and will be very difficult and unpleasant to eat.

If this happens, it's best to remove the radish, and put it on your compost heap.

How to harvest radishes

Harvesting your radishes is very easy. For the summer radishes you don't need any tools, they can just be pulled straight out the ground. When harvesting winter radishes, you may need a trowel, because they the soil will be firmer and winter radishes tend to be longer.

You don't need to harvest them all in one go, little and often is always best.

Start at one end of your row of radishes and carefully push the leaves to one side, so you can see the radish in the soil. Radishes are best harvested when the top of the radish is about 1-1.5 inches across. But they can be harvest when they are slightly smaller or larger.

Once you have chosen which radish you are going to harvest, hold the leaves at the point where they join the swollen radish root, and pull firmly.

If you are unable to pull your radish out of the ground you will need to use a trowel to loosen the soil. Push the trowel into the soil quite close to the radish, then pull the trowel back to open up the soil. You should them be able to pull out your radish very easily.

Once you have harvested the radishes you want, give the

remaining plants a good water. This will help the soil settle back around the remaining radishes.

HOW TO STORE RADISHES

Radishes are best eaten straight away, but if you have to store them here's what you need to do.

When you harvest your radishes, wash them thoroughly to clean off any dirt. Shake them dry and then put them in a clear plastic bag and store in the fridge for up to 1 week.

Radishes will not keep for much longer, and will then start to shrivel up and go hard.

Because radishes don't have much of a shelf life, only harvest what you need. This is why it's important to only sow short rows at a time, so you will always have fresh radish whenever you need them.

PREPARING YOUR RADISHES

I think the best way to eat radishes is raw.

When preparing a salad, slice your radishes very thinly, and scatter them in with the rest of the salad.

There are many different varieties of radishes and they come in many different shapes, sizes, and colours. Some radishes are white inside, where as others are the same colour inside as their skin.

If you have grown a good selection of radish, they will add plenty of different colours to your dishes, as well as crunch, and a peppery flavour.

When your salad is prepared, sprinkle with some sea salt and freshly ground pepper, and sprinkle on some freshly chopped chives.

Radishes are the taste of summer, and are a perfect accompaniment to any summer meal.

If you are having a summer party and want to show off your artistic skills, you can always make radish roses and place them around food on serving plates.

I don't have the artistic skills, or the patients to make a radish rose, so I'll leave it to the experts!

STRAWBERRIES

INTRODUCTION

Strawberries are hardy perennials, which means they grow larger every year. A strawberry plant will last for many years, although after about 4 years it won't produce much fruit.

I like to call strawberries the "Jewels of the Summer", because they look like red precious stones glistening through the green fruit bed.

> You know when summer has definitely arrived, because you start to harvest the first of your strawberries from your garden or allotment.

The strawberry season is short but sweet, lasting about 6 weeks from about the middle of June. But you can elongate your strawberry season by planting a variety of plants, where the fruit ripens at different rates. If you are very smart, you can be harvesting strawberries all summer long, and possibly into early Autumn.

In this book I will take you through each step, from sowing your seeds, letting you know how best to look after your growing plants, what pests and diseases to look out for, and then finally when to harvest your delicious, sweet, ripe fruits.

Harvesting your first ripe strawberry, which has been warmed by the sun, makes your fruits so sweet and flavourful. How many actually make it in the house for the rest of the family to try for pudding is difficult to say, as you'll keep nibbling them when you get a little peckish in your fruit patch.

Different types of strawberries

Strawberries come in five different types: Early, mid-season, late-season, everbearers (sometimes known as remontant or perpetual) and alpine (wild).

They all need to be looked after in exactly the same way, but their fruits will ripen at slightly different times. If you plant some of each variety, then you will elongate your strawberry season, so you will be able to enjoy fresh strawberries all summer long.

Let me talk you through each of the 5 types in a bit more detail, and give suggestions for my favourite varieties.

EARLY SEASON STRAWBERRIES

These will ripen from the middle of June, and continue to produce fruit until early July. There are many different varieties of early strawberries, but I would recommend "Malling Centenary", "Christine" or "Sweetheart."

These all have excellent flavour and the fruits are plump and delicious. They are best grown in full sun, but will grow very well if a little shade comes over them for a small part of the day. They'll produce fruit for about 3-4 years before production decreases and finally stops, so make sure you save the runners and re-pot them, so you'll never have to buy strawberry plants again.

Mid-season strawberries

These will be ripe and ready to eat from late June, through to the middle of July. So just as your early season strawberries are finishing, your mid-season plants will start fruiting.

There are so many varieties to choose from, depending on what size and flavour you are after, but I would recommend you try either "Elegance", "Royal Sovereign", or "Elsanta".

These produce large, firm strawberries, which have excellent flavour and a long shelf life. To get the best flavour from your strawberries they must have as much sun shining on them as possible.

> Pick a sunny part of the garden or allotment and they will thrive. Just like the early variety of strawberries, you'll get 3 or 4 summers of good fruit out of them, and then the plants will get old, and not produce much fruit.

You need to pot up the runners as they appear. Runners are new plants that grow from the adult plant. Then when the old plants have finished fruiting, you'll have new plants to replace them.

Late season strawberries

If you decide to grow these strawberries they will fruit throughout July and into the early part of August. With the sun still very high in the sky and long, warm and sunny days still a plenty, these fruits will be full of all that wonderful sweet strawberry flavour that we all crave.

I would recommend that you give either "Malwina", "Fenella" or "Florence" a try.

> All these strawberries have a deep, juicy strawberry flavour, with excellent sized fruits, and are the perfect way to round off the strawberry season.

Full sun is very important to get the sweet flavour in your strawberries, so pick a sunny spot and your strawberries will be very happy. You will get 3 or 4 years worth of good fruit out of each plant, then the fruit production will slow down as the plant gets old.

Replace any of the old plants with new plants, by re-potting the runners as they grow from the previous years.

Everbearers or perpetual strawberries

These strawberry plants will produce fruits throughout the summer, but in small quantities each time. So after their first flourish of fruits, just give them a little bit of time, feed and water them, and then they will produce another load of fruit a couple of weeks later. They will keep producing small amounts of fruit throughout the summer months, and into the autumn. The first frost will stop any more fruits from forming.

The fruits on the everbearing strawberries are a little smaller than the early, mid, and late season strawberries, but are still full of sweet strawberry flavour.

I would recommend the following varieties "Albion", "Buddy" or "Flamenco".

These strawberries will grow best in full sun, so make sure you choose the perfect spot for them. You'll get your best fruits from these plants on the second and third years. By the time the plants are into their forth year, the fruit production will have slowed down quite considerably. Dig up the old plants and replace with new plants that you made from the runners the previous year.

Alpine or wild strawberries

These are very, very tough strawberry plants, and can grow in partial shade. If they have space under a sheltered part of your garden, or by your shed, they will grow there very well. They make excellent ground cover, so are perfect for edging borders with. The fruits are fairly small, but don't let that put you off. The fruits have a great concentrated flavour and are usually red, but sometimes you get varieties that have white or yellow fruits. Although the yellow and white varieties can be a little hard to find.

Alpine strawberry plants produce fruit from early Summer through to late Autumn. Although they only produce fruits for 1 year. The plants don't die, but continue to grow, but will not produce any fruits. They are also the easiest strawberries to grow from seed, but you must sow your seeds in the early Autumn (end of September) and then transplant outside in the following Spring.

If you want to grow alpine strawberries I would recommend the following varieties: "Alexandra", "Golden Alexandra" and "Mignonette".

What are bare rooted strawberry plants?

Bare rooted plants is one of those terms that sometimes confuses people, so let me explain.

When you buy plants in a garden centre, they come in a pot with compost. If you buy several, they are usually put in a box or a bag for you so you can transport them home. When you get home you may notice that some of the soil has spilled out of the pot and gone everywhere.

With this in mind, it is impossible to send plants through the post this way.

Therefore the easiest way to send plant through the post is without the pot and also without most of the compost. These are called bare rooted plants, because their "roots are bare" of any compost.

Bare rooted plants are usually tied together either with an elastic band or string, put in a sealed cellophane bag with a little damp compost, which keeps the plants alive during transportation. They may also be wrapped in some damp paper to help keep the roots moist.

Once your plants arrive at your house, you must remove them from their packaging, and their tie, and plant them straight away either in the soil, raised bed or large pot. If you have to plant your strawberries in individual 3 inch pots because you only have a little time to spare, make sure that this is only a temporary place and the roots of the plants will need to spread out and grow.

If you leave the plants in the cellophane bag, they will go mouldy, and then you will lose the lot.

Many online companies send a variety of plants as bare rooted. Trees are usually sent this way as well, because it makes them much lighter to transport.

Seeds versus bare rooted plants

Strawberries can be bought as bare rooted plants or planted from seed, but which is best?

Growing strawberry plants from seed is very difficult, but not impossible. You need to be very patient, because germination can take up to 6 weeks.

You won't get fruit on your plants until their second year, and then only a few fruits. You'll have to wait until the following year for your strawberries to really produce those wonderful sweet strawberries.

I prefer to buy bare rooted plants, even though they are more expensive to start with, you haven't wasted a couple of years before they reward you with fruit. They are very easy to get, and all the hard work of looking after the growing plants is all done for you. Most of the bare rooted plants are taken from runners from other plants and not grown from seed.

You can of course go and buy strawberry plants from a garden centre, but they are much more expensive than buying bare rooted plants, and are no further along.

WHEN TO SOW STRAWBERRY SEEDS

Different types of strawberries are sown at different times. If you are sowing alpine strawberry seeds, then the seeds should be sown in early autumn until late September.

But if you are growing any of the other types of strawberries from seed, then these can be sown during the winter months, so between December to late February. If you sow your seeds in December, then you may get a few fruits in the summer, but if you sow your seeds in February then you are less likely to get any fruits the first year.

Personally, I would prefer to sow my strawberry seeds in February, then the plants can mature for 18 months before they produce their first fruits.

Strawberries need an even temperature to germinate. The ideal temperature is between 18-24 degrees celsius. If the temperature in your greenhouse is much colder that this, then your seeds will take much longer to germinate.

It might be worth starting your strawberry seeds off on a sunny window sill, inside your house, if the temperature where you live is too cold.

How to sow strawberry seeds

Strawberry seeds are tiny. Make sure that you are away from the slightest breeze when you sow them, otherwise you'll open the seed packet, tip the seeds in the palm of your hand, and the breeze will blow them away before you can even blink.

> Sowing strawberry seeds is quite easy, but you must make sure that you remember a few key things:

Get a seed tray, and fill it nearly to the top with multi purpose compost. If there are any lumps in the compost remove them. The compost must be very fine.

Very gently pat down the compost, just to make it even. Then, using a watering can with a rose on the end, water the compost. This will get rid of any air bubbles that are in the compost and level it off a little more.

Wait for the water to drain right through the compost, and then very carefully, using your thumb and forefinger, take a pinch of seeds, and sprinkle them over the damp compost.

> Try not to get too many seeds clustered together, although it's very hard to see the seeds once they have fallen on the compost.

Because the seeds are so tiny they only need a very tiny amount of compost sprinkled on top of them. So it's best to sieve the compost through a fine mesh. You only want to just cover the seeds with the thinnest layer of compost.

Label the seed tray, making sure you write down the variety and type of strawberries you've just sown.

There is no need to water again until the compost is dry. When you do water, make sure you use a fine spray so the water doesn't push the seeds too deep into the compost, or dislodge any of the emerging roots.

THE FIRST STRAWBERRY LEAVES

Your strawberry seedlings can take anywhere between 1-6 weeks to grow, and the first thing you will notice is a very thin green stem growing up with 2 oval leaves opening at the top. These are the plant's baby leaves and are very different from all the other leaves that will appear. Soon the baby leaves will shrivel and fall off. Don't worry about this.

The next set of leaves that appear are also oval in shape, but instead they have 5 points on the top edge. They'll look like a very small open fan.

As your strawberry plant grows, more fan-like leaves will appear, but will have more points on them, and gradually the leaves will get larger and their points more prominent.

All the leaves will grow out from the same central place at the base of the strawberry plant, this is called "the crown".

Potting up your strawberry seedlings

After your seedlings have been growing for about 3 or 4 weeks, they will need to be transplanted into individual 3 inch pots. Your plants will still be small and delicate, so be very careful when you prick them out and move them.

Don't leave your strawberry seedlings out of the soil for any longer than is necessary, as they will very quickly start to wilt. If the seedlings are out of the soil for too long they may die. So before you start to prick the seedlings out, make sure that you have all the 3 inch pots ready.

Fill each 3 inch pot right to the top with multi purpose compost, and gently pat down the compost, so that the top is level.

Using your middle finger, make a hole in the centre of the compost and push your finger down about 2 inches. Now you are ready to prick out your strawberry seedling.

This is a delicate operation, and must be done with great care. I have tried using many objects to prick out my seedlings, and find that a blunt pencil works the best.

Decide which seedling you are going to remove, and using the nib end of your pencil, carefully push the blunt end into the compost. Make sure that you leave a space of about 1 inch between the stem of the seedling and the nib of the pencil.

Push the pencil into the compost as far as you can, and then wiggle the pencil underneath the seedling and carefully lift the seedling up and out. It should come out fairly easily with its root ball, with some compost attached as well.

Then lower the seedling into the hole that you have made in the 3 inch pot, and fill in any gaps around the seedling with more compost.

Strawberries don't have a deep root system, so are very particular about how far down in the soil they want to be planted. You must make sure they are not planted too deep in the soil.

The roots must be in the soil, but the crown must be above the soil. If you plant them correctly they'll be very happy.

Once you have transplanted all your strawberry seedlings, put the 3 inch pots on a tray, and put water in the tray. Let the compost in the pots soak up the soil, as this will encourage the roots of the plants to grow downwards. Water only when all the water in the tray has gone, and the soil on the top of the 3 inch pots looks a little dry. Strawberries don't like to sit in really wet soil all the time. If the compost is too wet for too long, then the crown will rot.

Your seedling will need to stay in these 3 inch pots for at least another couple of months, until they are large enough to be transplanted outside into the soil.

Planting out your strawberries

A strawberry plant has 4 main parts: the roots, the crown (where the leaves grow from), the leaves and the fruit.

Once your strawberry plants are about 5-6 inches tall, they will be ready to plant outside. Make sure you acclimatise your plants for about 7 days before you plant them outside. Remember they have been growing in a protected environment, so they may go into shock if the conditions they are used to suddenly change.

To acclimatise your plants, place them outside in your garden in a sheltered spot during the day, and then bring them back inside overnight.

Strawberries can be grown in the open ground, in hanging baskets, in a strawberry barrel, in raised beds or in a variety of different sized pots. To be honest, they will grow anywhere.

Let me run through each of these, as there are a few things you need to think about before you decide which is best for you.

Open ground

If you are planting your strawberries in the open ground, then space your plant at least 12 inches apart from each other, as this will give the plants plenty of room to grow.

Again make sure that you don't plant your strawberries too low in the soil. Remember the roots are below the soil, but the crown must be above the soil. Once you have planted all your strawberry plants, water them in well. Then water weekly throughout the summer and early autumn so they get well established. During a heatwave you may have to water your strawberries twice a week.

Strawberries like free draining soil, so if you have very heavy clay, then you may be better off growing your strawberries in one of the other options.

HANGING BASKETS

Make sure you don't over crowd your strawberries in hanging baskets. Fill the hanging basket, nearly to the top with multi purpose compost. Pat it down gently before planting your strawberries.

> Hanging baskets will need frequent watering as they don't hold the water very well. I would suggest you water your plants every day, but in a heat wave, you may have to water twice a day.

If you have a semi circle hanging basket, then I would only plant 2 plants, one on each side. The strawberries are very easy to harvest, and the plants will cascade over the side of the basket. They are a great way to make fencing look more attractive and interesting.

Circular hanging baskets vary in size, so my suggestion is for a hanging basket that measures 12 inches across. Again, fill the hanging basket nearly to the top with multi purpose compost and pat down gently. Plant 4 strawberry plants in the circular hanging basket, evenly spaced, and as close to the edge as you can. Water well, and then water every day, but twice a day during a heatwave. The fruits will cascade over the edge of the hanging basket and will be very easy to harvest.

> Growing strawberries in a hanging basket makes a very attractive addition to your garden, and a wonderful change from the usual flowers that are usually grown in them.

Strawberry barrel

These are a great idea if space is limited, as you can grow lots of plants in a very small space. They can be bought online or at a garden centre. They're usually plastic, and are about the size of a water butt, but smaller ones can be found. However, if you can find a wooden strawberry barrel, these are excellent, but they are more expensive. If you know someone who makes wooden barrels (a cooper), then maybe you could have one specially made?

> Before you fill your barrel, you must make sure there are drainage holes in the base. These holes, are best made using an electrical drill, and getting the largest drill bit you can find. Make as many holes as you like, the more the better.

Next, decide where you want your barrel to stand. I know this sounds an obvious thing, but once the barrel is filled you won't be able to move it. So it's important that you get it in place now. Strawberries like to grow in the sun, so find the sunniest place in your garden for them to grow. Don't put your barrel in a corner, because the plants at the back of the barrel won't see any sun at all, and will then die.

Place a layer of broken bricks and broken terracotta in the base of the barrel, as this will help with drainage. Then fill the rest of the barrel up with a mixture of well rotted manure, sand and multi purpose compost. The manure will feed the plants as they grow, and the sand will help with drainage. Fill the barrel right to the top and leave it to settle for a few days before you plant your strawberry plants.

Planting your strawberries in the barrel is very easy. Where the holes are round the outside of the barrel, scoop out enough soil, so you are able to get the roots of your strawberry plant in. Push the plant in firmly, and then fill in the gaps with more compost. The plants will cascade down the the barrel. On the very top of the barrel, plant your strawberries round the edge and in the centre. Space them about 12 inches apart from each other. This will give them plenty of room for their roots to spread and the plants to grow.

Watering the plants in your barrel can be a little time consuming, as you have to water each plant separately. Use a watering can with a thin spout, and water each plant, starting from the top and working your way down to the bottom.

Don't just water from the top of the barrel and assume the water will filter all the way down the barrel, because it won't.

Raised beds

Raised beds come in all sorts of different shapes and sizes. You can get some made to measure, but others come as a standard size.

If you decide that you are going to grow your strawberry plants in raised bed you need to fill your beds the same way.

In the very bottom of the raised bed put a thick layer of wood chips. This will help retain moisture deep down in the soil. Then fill the rest of the bed with mostly top soil, but add a little ballast (make sure there are small stones, but no cement in your ballast) and manure. The ballast will help with the drainage and the manure will feed the plants.

Fill the raised bed to the very top, and leave it to settle for at least a week. The level of the soil mixture will sink a couple of inches. Don't worry as this is normal.

Once the soil has settled, it's time to plant your strawberries. Whether you want them in perfect lines, or not, you need to make sure that you position your plants 12 inches apart from each other. Also make sure that the roots are below the soil, and the crown and leaves are above the soil.

Once you have planted your strawberries, give them a thorough water in. Water once a week until the autumn. If you have a heatwave, water twice a week. Then, the following year, just water once a week from early May until the end of summer. If you have a very hot April, then you will have to water your plants.

Pots

Strawberries will grow very happily in pots. It doesn't matter what size the pots are. You can have any pots from 6 inches across, to 6 feet across. You just need to make sure you give your plants enough room to grow and spread. Remember your plants need to be planted at least 12 inches apart from each other.

If you are growing your strawberries in pots, then you can place your pots wherever you like. If you only have 6 inch pots, then you could make a pyramid shape, with a solid structure underneath. This can look very eye catching and interesting, just let you imagination run wild with any structure you want to create.

Whatever size pots you use, your must make sure they have

drainage holes down the bottom, and then place in some crocks (either large stones or broken terracotta pots), then fill the remainder of the pot with a mixture of multi purpose compost, adding a little sand and manure as well.

With regards to watering your pots, it depends on their size. Smaller pots will need to be watered more frequently than larger pots, so check the soil in your pots daily, and if it seems dry, give them a water.

Always water from the top, so the water can drain downwards. Strawberry roots don't like to sit in wet soil for long.

Because strawberries have a very shallow root system, you can grow them anywhere. Why not try growing them in an old pair of wellingtons, or shoes. But make sure you have some good drainage holes in the sole of the footwear, and before you fill them with compost, put in some stones or broken up terracotta to aid drainage. If you have some guttering, attach it to the side of some fencing or your shed. But again make sure you put drainage holes in before you put the compost in.

Strawberry runners

Strawberry plants send out runners, no they don't have shorts and trainers on. Strawberry runners are the new plants for the following year.

They grow from the crown of the adult plant, and start off as a long green stem. After about a week, you'll notice small leaves growing at the end of the stem, and then as the weeks go by the leaves will get larger, and then roots will start to grow below the leaves. Once the new plant has roots, it can send out another runner and so the process starts again.

One strawberry plant can send out over 6 runners for the adult plants crown. So if you've only bought half a dozen plants the first year, and if you save all your runners the first summer, you could end up with over 30 plants the following summer.

Runners are sent out all summer long, but take a lot of energy away from the adult plant, so it'll produce less fruit. I would suggest that you cut of any runners that appear while the plant is fruiting and discard them. Once the plant has finished fruiting then allow the runners to grow.

As the new runners grow, it's very easy to encourage them to grow into little 3 inch pots.

Fill a small pot, right to the top with multipurpose compost and gently pat it down. As the new strawberry plants start to produce roots, then rest the new plant on top of the compost. The roots will grow down into the compost and you'll have a new plant.

When the new plant is a good size and the root system is strong, you can then cut the new plant off from the adult plant.

The stem of the runner has been feeding the new plant, but once the new plant is established it can survive on it's own. Just cut the stem near the base of the new plant and then you can move the new plant wherever you want.

You can transplant the new plants straight into the soil, raised bed, or container, but make sure you water the new plant in well, so the plant gets established in its new home quickly. You should get a few fruits from it the following summer.

HOW TO LOOK AFTER YOUR STRAWBERRY PLANTS AS THEY GROW

Strawberry plants are very easy to look after and are perfect if you are a beginner at gardening, or want something low maintenance to look after, and they're great for children to grow.

Watering

Make sure that when you first plant your strawberries you water them in very well, and always water from above so the roots don't sit in wet soil for too long.

If you are growing your strawberries in the open ground or a large raised bed, water them once a week until they stop fruiting. They shouldn't need watering again until the following spring. If however, you have a very hot autumn, you will have to continue to water them until the temperature cools down. If you have a summer heatwave, then you will need to water them twice a week.

If you are growing your strawberries in a container of some sort, again water them in thoroughly when you plant them out.

Then water at least twice a week until they stop fruiting. If the autumn is still hot, then continue to water until the temperature cools. If you have a heatwave, then you may have to water your strawberries every day. The soil in small pots will dry out very quickly, so keep checking your pots, and if the soil seems dry then water them.

Always water your strawberries from above, using a watering can with a spray attachment. That way the water will go directly down into the soil, and to the plant's roots.

Feeding

Strawberries will need feeding once the flowers start to appear. I feed mine with Shropshire Seaweed Fertiliser. This can be used every time you water your plants. Just add a small amount to your watering can once you added the water, stir, and then water away. The instructions are on the bottle. If you use this, your fruits will grow beautifully, and taste so sweet, and not at all of seaweed.

If you don't have Shropshire Seaweed fertiliser, then normal fruit feed will work fine, but follow the instructions on the bottle.

PESTS AND DIASEASES

There aren't many problems that will befall your wonderful strawberries, but there are a few I would suggest you watch out for.

Slugs

Yes, these horrors will attack your wonderful, sweet strawberries. They love the taste of the ripe fruits. You'll know when your strawberries have been attacked by slugs, because you will find holes on your strawberries. Slugs tend not to eat the entire fruit, just a bit. You can still harvest the fruits and eat them. But cut away the munched out bit and cut your strawberries in pieces. Make sure you wash your strawberries very throughly.

Slugs tend not to each the leaves of your plants, but like to hide in the dark, damp areas below the leaves.

The best way to stop the slugs from attacking your fruits is to make sure you regularly clear out any debris on the soil, remove and brown leaves and spread a thick layer of straw round the base of each plant. Straw is prickly and the slugs don't like it.

Mice

Mice also love ripe strawberries, and will destroy your crop very fast. You'll know if you have mice in your strawberry patch, because you'll notice that fruits suddenly disappear and all that is left is a tiny amount of the top of the strawberry attached to the stem. Fortunately mice aren't that common, unless you live in the heart of the country. But if you do suspect mice, then you'll need to mouse-proof your strawberry area. The best way to do this is to run a very fine wire mesh around your strawberry area. Make sure that you hide some of the mesh under the soil. The holes of the mesh must be very tiny, as mice can squeeze through very small spaces. If you suspect that you have some trapped in your strawberry bed, then lay some humane traps to catch them in and then you can release them back out into the wild.

Mouldy fruits

Strawberries are very delicate, and can be damaged very easily. If you squeeze the fruits too hard they will bruise, and any bruised fruits will go mouldy in a couple of days. So you must be very careful when handling your fruits.

A heavy rain shower will also bruise the fruits. This is very difficult to predict, so placing a thick layer of straw under the fruits will help. If heavy rain is forecast, add a thin layer of straw over the top of the fruits, will also help protect most of your fruits from getting damaged by the rain. You will still get some damage to your fruits, but most of them will be saved.

WHEN TO HARVEST YOUR STRAWBERRIES

Most strawberries are red when they need to be harvested. But that's not always the case. This is how to tell when your strawberries are ready to harvest.

Red strawberries

Red strawberries will start off green in colour, and as they grow, and the sun shines on them they will ripen to a wonderful shiny, bright red colour.

When the entire strawberry is red, then it is ready to harvest. Check all round the strawberry before you harvest it, as sometimes the underside of the strawberry may still be green. If this is the case, just leave the strawberry to ripen for another day and then check again.

Sometimes, the very top of the strawberry, where it meets the green stem, stays white. This is quite normal. If this happens you can still harvest your strawberries.

White strawberries

If you are growing white strawberries, these are often called "Pineberries" or "Snow white" and have a unique pineapple/strawberry flavour. They tend to be a little more expensive than red strawberries. But you treat them exactly the same as you would the red strawberries.

White strawberries don't start off green, but white, and as they grow and ripen you'll notice that the flesh of the strawberry turns a slight pink colour and the seeds will turn red. When this happens, your white strawberries are ready to harvest.

HOW TO HARVEST YOUR STRAWBERRIES

Harvesting your strawberries is very easy, but you must be careful, as the fruits will bruise very easily. Hold the strawberry in the palm of your hand, and cup your hand around it. Then, using the nails on your thumb and forefinger, pinch off the stem. And there you have it, your first strawberry.

Harvest all the ripe fruits you can find, and either eat them straight away, make some jam, scones or pies, or any other delicious treats you like. But strawberries will keep in the fridge for a few of days.

> Check your strawberry plants every couple of days as they will ripen very quickly and you won't want to miss any.

You can also freeze strawberries. Place them in one layer on a baking tray and put them in the freezer. Once they are frozen, place them in a freezer bag. When you want to eat some, take out what you need and place in a bowl to defrost. They will release some juice, so make sure your bowl is deep enough to hold the juice. Defrosted frozen strawberries are a bit soft, but still have their wonderful flavour and are perfect on cereal.

STRAWBERRY RECIPE

Strawberries are best eaten as soon as possible, but you can make them even more delicious.

Ingredients

- Fresh strawberries, enough for 4 people
- 4 tablespoons of icing sugar
- 4 table spoons of framboise liqueur, raspberry flavour (optional)
- A small pot of creme fraiche

Method

1. Take the green stems off the strawberries, wash and dry them, and place them in a bowl.
2. Make sure the strawberries are roughly the same size. You may have to cut some of them up.
3. Pour the framboise over the strawberries and carefully

give them a stir. If you are not using this, just miss this step out.

4. Sprinkle the icing sugar over the strawberries, cover will cling film and place in the fridge for between 30 - 60 minutes. The icing sugar will encourage the juices to come out of the strawberries and make a wonderful sauce.
5. Spoon your strawberries into individual bowls and add a blob of creme fraiche on top.

TOMATOES

INTRODUCTION

Tomatoes are a fruit and not a vegetable, as many people think. They can be grown outside in a garden, or on an allotment, or even in a hanging basket. They can also be grown in a greenhouse, poly tunnel and even in a conservatory.

Not long after Mark and I got married we lived in a one bedroom ground floor flat with a small conservatory, and I grew my tomato plants in the conservatory. They grew beautifully and I harvested so many wonderfully large plum red tomatoes that it made our landlady very jealous.

Now I grow some outside and others I grow in my greenhouse. Wherever you grow your tomatoes you need to look after in the same way, although some may need a little more watering than others.

Freshly harvested tomatoes are amazing. They are warm, juicy, and so full of flavour. You just can't find anything like them in shops. The shop-bought tomatoes are flavourless, even those that are still on the vine have very little flavour. Nothing compares to tomatoes you have grown yourself.

If you've never tried growing tomatoes before but have always wanted to, this book will give you everything you need to know.

DIFFERENT TYPES OF TOMATOES

Cordon, bush, or somewhere in the middle

Tomatoes come in three types: cordon (or indeterminate), bush (determinate), or a little in between the two (semi determinate). Let me explain about each of these.

Cordon or indeterminate

These tomatoes can grow up to six foot tall and will need support from a structure. There are several structures that you can use, we all have our favourites, but I find the following works best for me.

You can either use a metal pole, or you can make a long ridge structure out of bamboo canes. Whatever you decide to do, make sure each pole or cane is 18 inches apart from the other. This will allow the air to circulate round each plant, and also allow the roots of the plant to spread, and therefore the plant to bush out and grow well.

Make sure that your poles or canes are firmly pushed into the soil at least nine inches, or further if you can. Only plant one tomato plant per cane or pole.

Once the plants start to produce tomatoes the weight of the growing tomatoes can make your tomato plants fall over. So you must make sure you attach your plants to your structure very securely using garden twine.

Bush or determinate

Bush tomatoes are exactly that; they grow into a bush. They don't need any structure to support them as they grow, and are perfect for growing in raised beds and hanging baskets. Grow one plant per hanging basket, but if you're growing them in a raised bed plant them about 12 inches apart from each other.

A little in between, or semi determinate

There aren't many of these about, and they won't grow as tall as the cordon plants and will only get up to a maximum of 5 foot tall, and will be a little on the bushy side. They will need to be supported by a stake of some kind, just like the cordon tomatoes. These will also need to be planted about 18 inches apart from each other. This will give them plenty of room for the roots to grow and spread, and also allow the air to circulate round the plants. They will also need to be tied onto their support with garden twine.

DIFFERENT SIZES OF TOMATOES

Beefsteak, standard, cherry

Tomatoes come in three different sizes: beefsteak, standard and cherry. They all need the same attention given to them as they grow. Let me tell you about each one.

Beefsteak

These are the very large tomatoes, that can be the size of your entire hand. One beefsteak tomato can weigh more that one pound in weight! They look amazing when they are growing on the plant, and may need a little bit of support to stop the main stem bending over.

The best way to support them is to use a pair of old stockings or tights, and make a hammock for the tomatoes to rest on.

Attach the ends of the stocking to something sturdy, for example greenhouse staging. Like all tomatoes they grow on a “truss”. A “truss” is a branch that comes out from the main stem and the tomatoes grow from it. You may only have about 3 or 4 tomatoes growing from each truss.

Before you eat your beefsteak tomatoes, you will need to remove the little section at the top of the tomato where it joined onto the plant, as this is very hard.

If you are growing beefsteak tomatoes, I would recommend from “Black Krim”, or “Bountiful F1”.

Standard

These are the most popular size of tomatoes and are either round or oval and are about 2-3 inches across. The standard size, are the most common ones you’ll find in the shops. These tomatoes also grow from a “truss”, and you will have anywhere between 8-12 tomatoes growing from each truss.

These tomatoes don’t usually need supporting by a hammock, but if they do, again the best way is to use a stocking or an old pair of tights.

Before you eat these tomatoes, you don’t have to cut out the little section where the tomato joins the plant because it’s not tough. Just slice, or cut the tomatoes into quarters. If you are growing standard tomatoes I would recommend from “Alicante” or “Green Zebra.”

Cherry

These are little tiny tomatoes, and are perfect for just picking and popping straight in your mouth. They can be round or oval and will grow to about 1 inch in diameter, but sometimes they are smaller. Cherry tomatoes also grow from a truss, but their trusses can be very long, with a few dozen tomatoes growing on each truss. These tomatoes won't need supporting with a hammock as they are not heavy enough.

When you harvest your cherry tomatoes, all you need to do is to give them a quick rinse under the tap. They don't need cutting, just pick, rinse and eat.

If you are growing cherry tomatoes, I would suggest from "Gartenperle" or "Tumbling Tom Yellow". Some cherry tomatoes grow from a compact bush plant, where as others grow from tumbling plants. These are best grown in a hanging basket, as they can then cascade over the basket and downwards.

WHEN TO SOW YOUR TOMATOES

Tomato seeds are one of the first seeds that you sow at the beginning of the year. They must be sown either in a greenhouse, polytunnel, cold frame or on a sunny window sill.

In the UK they must never be sown outside in the soil. The seeds are too small, and our climate is too cold. Even where my parents live in Spain, my mum sows them inside.

If you have a heated greenhouse or a sunny window sill, then you can sow your tomato seeds as early as January. But if you're growing them in an unheated greenhouse or cold frame, then wait until the middle of February to the middle of March to sow your tomato seeds.

Wherever you sow your tomato seeds, they will all benefit from a propagator lid being placed on top of the seed tray. This will help keep in the moisture as well as the heat, and your seeds will germinate a little faster.

Propagator lids are available to buy from most garden centre and DIY stores. They are usually the size that will fit the standard seed tray, but smaller ones can be found. If you are sowing your seeds in a small 3 inch pot and not a seed tray, then placing a clear plastic bag over the top of your pot will work perfectly well. Just seal it securely with an elastic band. Whatever propagator lid you use, make sure that it fits snuggly.

HOW TO SOW YOUR TOMATOES

Wherever you decide to grow your tomatoes, be it in a greenhouse, cold frame, or on a window sill, they all need to be sown exactly the same way.

Fill your seed tray or small pot nearly to the top with multipurpose compost and then gently pat the compost down to make it level. Water the compost from above, using a watering can with a rose on the end. Watering the compost from the top will get rid of any air pockets that may be in the compost, and the compost will settle a little further. Wait for all the water to drain from the top of the compost before you start to sow your tomato seeds.

The amount of seeds you get per pack, depends on what variety you choose. You tend to find that the most popular varieties have more seeds per packet.

The germination rate for tomatoes is usually very good, so if you only want to end up with about six tomato plants, I would suggest you sow about eight seeds.

Carefully sprinkle your seeds on top of the damp compost, making sure none of the seeds are touching each other. Then sprinkle a little more compost over the seeds, so the seeds are just covered. Don't pat this bit of compost down, otherwise the germinating seeds won't be able to break through as they grow.

Make sure you label your seed tray, and also mark down whether your tomatoes are beefsteak, standard or cherry tomatoes, or cordon or bush. If you don't do it now, you'll forget what you planted, and when it's time to plant your tomatoes out in early summer you won't remember.

Cover your seed tray with a propagator lid and don't water again until the compost is drying out. But water sparingly and from the top, because if the seeds get too wet they will rot and won't germinate.

THE FIRST LEAVES

It can take a few weeks, sometimes longer for your tomato seeds to start germinating, so be patient. Tomato seeds need a little bit of warmth to germinate, so starting them off in a warm and protected environment helps them germinate much faster.

The stems will emerge first from the seed, and will push through the soil. They don't emerge in a straight line, but in an arch. What you will notice first are little green arches popping through the soil. Don't be tempted to try and straighten them up, just water gently, and give them a couple more days to straighten up. The leaves are the last part to emerge from the seed, and once they have appeared, then the plant will straighten up.

The first leaves are long and thin, they don't look like all the other tomato leaves. As the plant grows, these first leaves will shrivel and drop off. The rest of the leaves that grow will all then look like the tomatoes leaves we know. They will be bright green, and as long as the plant is looked after well, they will stay green, until near the end of the tomatoes' life in October time.

POTTING ON YOUR TOMATOES

As your tomatoes grow they will need more space to spread their roots out, so you will need to transplant them into larger pots.

When your tomato seedlings are about 2-3 inches tall, they will be strong and sturdy enough to be moved. But you must still be very gentle with them, as they are still very small.

When you transplant your seedling from their seed tray to individual pots, they must go from their seeds tray to their new pot quickly. Don't leave them lying out of the compost, because they will go dry and die. So before you start pricking out your tomato seedlings, make sure your have prepared the pots they're going to go into first.

The best sized pots to transplant your tomato seedlings into are 3.5 inch pots, these can be bought very easily from most garden centres. Fill the pot right to the top with multi purpose compost, and gently press down. Then get your finger, and make a hole in the very centre of the compost. Push your finger down as far as it'll go.

Now you need to get out a seedling. This takes time, and don't rush, because if you're not careful, you'll damage your seedlings. If you break a seedling, it can't be mended. The best way to remove your seedlings from their tray is to use a blunt pencil.

Decide which seedling you want to remove. Then, using your pencil carefully, push the blunt pencil into the soil, about an inch away from the seedling you want to remove. Then using the pencil like a spoon, scoop up the seedling, its roots and some of the compost it's been growing in. The seedling should then lift up very easily, and then you can gently move it to it's larger pot.

Some people say to hold the seedling by the leaves, but if there is a clod of compost on the roots, then the seedling will break. I just hold it very gently round the stem and rest it in my hand.

Move the seedling over to the pot and compost that you have prepared, and place the roots and most of the stem into the hole. Let gravity take the seedling down into the hole, make sure you don't push it in, otherwise the seedling will break.

Once the seedling is in the hole as far is it will go, carefully fill in any space round the seedling with more compost, put the pot in a tray and water from the base. This will encourage the roots to grow downwards and fill the pot.

Only choose the strongest seedlings to transplant. Any that are very small, or are disfigured put on the compost heap.

As your tomatoes grow, they will need watering, but make sure you don't over-water them, especially at this early stage, as they don't like to sit in wet soil all the time. Water them little and often, and only when the compost looks a little dry. Your tomatoes will grow in their 3.5 inch pots for about 6-8 weeks, and once the weather starts to warm up they will grow very fast.

PLANTING OUT YOUR TOMATOES

Your tomato plants need to be kept undercover, in a greenhouse or cold frame until all frost has gone from your area.

In the south of the UK, tomatoes can be planted out in early June. For the middle part of the UK, tomatoes can be planted out in the middle of June. And in the northern part of the UK, tomatoes can be planted out at the end of June. These are only rough times, so please watch your weather forecast as you may be able to get your plants outside a week or two earlier if no frost is due in your area.

If you are planting your tomato plants outside, a couple of weeks beforehand, you must acclimatise your plants to the outside temperature. Remember they have been growing in a very calm environment away from the wind and the rain. If you suddenly change that environment, then the plants will go into shock, and will either stop growing, or possibly die.

To acclimatise your plants, move them out into a sheltered part of your garden during the day. Leave them outside all day, and then, just before the sun is about to set, move them back into their protected environment. If the day is likely to be wet and windy, then keep your plants inside until the weather has calmed down.

Acclimatising your plants toughens them up, and when you do plant them outside in the soil they will continue to grow and won't go into shock.

When you plant your tomatoes outside there are a few things that you need to remember. If you are planting out bush varieties, make sure you give them enough room to spread their roots. If you are growing bush varieties in a hanging basket, only grow one plant per hanging basket. This will allow the plants to reach their full potential and also get enough water. If you are planting bush varieties out in a raised bed, then make sure they are at lease 12 inches apart from each other. Sprinkle around the base of each plant some slug protection. You'll only need to do this once, and very soon the plants will be too big for the slugs and snails to bother with.

If you are growing either of the cordon varieties, again these need enough room for their roots to spread out. Each plant should be planted 15-18 inches apart form each other.

You need to make sure that they are firmly planted in the soil, because if they are not, then they will fall over due to the weight of the fruits growing one their trusses.

Using a hand trowel, dig a hole a little wider and a little deeper that the pot the tomato plant is growing in. To remove the tomato plant from the pot, makes sure you support the stem of the tomato plant using two fingers, and turn the tomato plant upside down. Take the bottom of the pot and you should be able to remove the pot easily.

Place the tomato plant in the hole, and fill in around the plant with more soil. Firmly push the soil down to make sure the plant is in place.

You will then need to support both cordon varieties as they grow. Using either a bamboo cane or a metal support. Insert the support into the soil, about two inches from the stem of the tomato plant. Make sure you push the supporting pole down as far as you can, and that it's very secure in the soil. You will need to get a support that is at least 6 or 7 feet long.

Once the support is in place, using some garden twine, and carefully tie the tomato plant to the support.

Water the plants in and sprinkle a little slug protection around the base of each plant. You will only need to do this once, because soon the plant will be too big for the slugs and snails to bother with.

If you are growing your tomatoes in a greenhouse or poly tunnel, then the best way to do this is to use either grow bags, or large pots.

GROW BAGS

A grow bag is filled with multipurpose compost, and they can be bought very easily from your local garden centre or DIY store. If you are using a grow bag, lay the bag flat on the ground. You will need to make some drainage holes in the bottom of the bag, and the best way to do this is to use a large screwdriver.

On the top of the grow bag, you will need to use scissors to cut three evenly spaced holes in which to plant your tomatoes. Sometimes these are marked out on the bag.

Make sure the holes are just large enough to plant your tomatoes in the compost. If you make the holes too large, every time you water your tomato plants, you'll lose lots of the compost from the bag.

Once you have transplanted your tomatoes into the grow bag, then insert their support and water. You won't be able to put the support down far enough to make it sturdy, so you'll have to attach the support the your greenhouse or polytunnel staging, or frame.

LARGE POTS

You can also grow your tomatoes in large pots. Make sure that the pots are at least 9 inches in diameter, larger if you have them. Remember, the roots of the tomato plants need to spread out.

If the pots are too small, then the roots can't spread out enough, and the plant will become pot bound. This will also affect the growth of the tomato plant, and it won't reach its full potential.

Fill each pot with multipurpose compost, and when you transplant your tomato plants into the large pots, make sure you firm more compost around them.

Again you will need to put in a support for your tomatoes, but these supports will have to be attached to staging or the frame of your greenhouse or polytunnel.

Water all your plants when you've transplanted them, and sprinkle something to deter the slugs. You'll only have to do this once, as the plants will grow rapidly and become too large for the slugs to eat.

Place the pots in deep trays, as they help retain the water.

HOW TO LOOK AFTER YOUR TOMATOES AS THEY GROW

Whether you're growing your tomatoes outside in the soil, or in a greenhouse they need the same care.

Watering

If you are growing your tomatoes outside in the soil they will need to be watered well.

Twice a week is sufficient. Use either a watering can, without a rose sprinkler on the end, or a hose, again without any attachment on the end. Watering this way will make sure the water goes directly into the soil and down to the roots. What you don't want is for the water to sit on top of the soil and then evaporate into the air and get wasted.

Water about 2 inches away from the stem of the tomato plant. This will encourage the roots to spread out and down to find the water, making the tomato plant much more stable and strong.

If you are growing your tomatoes in a greenhouse, then water the tray that the pots are sitting in. Only fill the trays halfway up. The compost in the pots will absorb the water, and the roots of the tomato plant will then grow downwards towards the water, and fill the pot. Don't add anymore water to the tray until the previous water has gone, otherwise it'll get stagnant and start to smell, and then bacteria may start to form and get into your tomato plants and kill them.

If you are growing your tomatoes in hanging baskets, they will need watering every other day. If the weather is really hot, they will need to be watered every day. Try watering at the end of the day, when the temperature is cooler. The soil will absorb the water and the plants will drink the water up overnight.

FEEDING

All tomatoes need feeding, wherever they grow. But make sure you don't feed them too early.

You should only start to feed your plants once the flowers have started to appear. If you start to feed them any earlier, all it will do is encourage the plant to produce loads more leaves. It's the flowers that need the extra feed and not the leaves.

You can buy all sorts of different feeds for your tomatoes, either in liquid form specifically for tomatoes, slow release tablets, or pellets, or general liquid plant feed. They also vary quite dramatically in price.

Over my years of growing many different varieties of tomatoes, I have tried many different types of feed for my tomatoes, and have come to the conclusion that the one that works best for me is Shropshire Seaweed Fertiliser. I've mentioned it in all my books so far, I think, and I'm sure I'll mention it in all the other ones I write.

It's a general fertiliser and is suitable for all plants. But unlike all the other feeds, which you can only give at certain times, Shropshire Seaweed Fertiliser can be given every time you water. So you'll never miss a feed.

I swear by it, and have been using it for several years now, and wouldn't use anything else.

SIDE SHOOTING

Not all tomatoes need to have their side shoots removed. If you are growing bush tomatoes they do **not** need side shooting. The fruits will come from the side shoots.

If you are growing the tall tomatoes or cordon, they will need their side shoots removed,. Side shoots grow very fast, and will take away the energy from the tomato plant, and it won't produce many tomatoes.

Where do you find the side shoot?

Follow the main stem, from the base of the plant, and work your way slowly up the plant. You will see a leaf stem coming off the main stem at about a 90 degree angle, and the side shoot will be growing in between the main stem and the leaf stem at about a 45 degree angle.

If the side shoot is small, then you can pinch it off with your nails, but if it is quite large, then you may have to cut with some scissors, or secateurs.

Keep checking your tomato plants at least once a week, because even though you have removed a side shoot another one will grow in it's place.

TYING IN YOUR TOMATOES

If you are growing cordon tomatoes, as they grow taller, they'll need to be tied securely to their supporting stake. This will stop the tomato plant from falling over and breaking. The best way to attach the plant to the support is by using some garden twine.

Do not use wire, as this could cut into the stem of the plant as it grows and could introduce disease into the plant.

When you attach the tomato to the support using twine, don't tie the twine too tightly around the tomato plant. The stem will need to swell as the plant grows, and if the twine is too tight the plant will be strangled.

Trusses

On cordon tomatoes, a truss is the branch where the tomatoes grow from.

It all depends on how many tomatoes you want to grow, but the ideal number of trusses per tomato plant is about 4-6. Once your tomato plant has produced enough trusses, then you can snip off the top of the tomato plant. This will make sure that the plant puts all its energy into ripening the tomatoes already growing on it, and not into producing more tomatoes.

Tomatoes are thirsty and hungry plants, so make sure they have enough feed and water, especially during very hot weather. But tomato roots don't like to sit in water for too long, so little and often is ideal, especially if you're growing in a greenhouse.

PESTS AND DISEASES

The tomato plants and their fruits can be attacked by a number of pests and diseases.

Some you are able to rectify very quickly, others you will need to destroy the plant or fruit immediately to stop it from spreading any further.

I will mention the most common pests or diseases that you may come across.

Blight

This is the most common disease, and one that all gardeners are always on the look out for. If you notice the slightest evidence of blight on one of your plants, it will very quickly spread to all the other tomato plants within days. Although blight is common, it can be prevented.

If your tomato or potato plants have suffered from blight one year, make sure that you don't plant any tomato or potato plants in the same area for at least 2 years.

Blight is a fungus and likes humid and damp conditions. So if the weather is hot and humid during the day, and with that sometimes comes rain, then be on the look out. This is why it is usually more prevalent during the end of the summer.

The first signs of blight on your tomato plants, will be small brown patches on either the stem of the plant or the edges of the leaves.

These brown patches will spread very quickly to the fruit. When I say quickly, I'm talking about a couple of days. You'll know the disease has got to your fruit because the tops of the tomatoes will start to go brown and shrivel up.

There is no cure for blight, even if you spot it early. The only thing you can do is to remove any effected plants and either burn them, or take them straight to the rubbish tip.

Under no circumstances should you put them on the compost heap as this will spread the disease further.

You can however save some of your fruits. As soon as you spot any blight on your plants, quickly harvest any fruit that is growing. Don't worry if the tomatoes are still green, they will soon ripen. Put any fruit you harvest on a metal tray and cover with a tea towel. Then place the tray of tomatoes in a kitchen cupboard or in the cupboard under the stairs. Check your tomatoes once a week and use the ripe ones immediately.

If any of the tomatoes on the tray start to show any sign of blight, then throw them away.

You can buy blight resistant or blight tolerant tomato seeds, but how good they are I can't confirm. I did try some once, years ago, and they didn't work. But that was many years ago, so they may be better now.

If you are growing your tomatoes under cover, either in a polytunnel or a greenhouse, then the likelihood of them getting blight is greatly reduced. Even though it is humid inside the greenhouse or polytunnel, there is not much water about that can sit on the leaves of the tomato plants.

It's the combination of the humid conditions and the damp that allows the blight fungus to grow.

If you only have one of those conditions, then the fungus can not grow. This is another reason why it is very important to water your tomato plants at the base, rather than using a hose with a spray on the end.

Magnesium Deficiency

If you notice that the leaves of your tomato plants are turning yellow, then this is likely to be a magnesium deficiency in the plant.

Make sure that you use a feed that contains magnesium. I would recommend that you use Shropshire Seaweed Fertiliser as this contains magnesium and if you feed your plants only this then they should be fine.

This is easily cured and your fruit will not suffer any ill effects.

Blossom End Rot

As your tomato grows, you may notice a small brown patch appear at the very base of your fruit. The brown patch will be hard and will create a concave area on your tomato.

Blossom end rot is caused by allowing the soil to get too dry too often.

Make sure that you water regularly. Remove any damaged fruits and throw away. Blossom end rot is more common when growing tomato plants in grow bags, because they will need more frequent watering. If the weather is very warm and the greenhouse or polytunnel gets very hot, you may have to water your tomatoes every other day to prevent blossom end rot from happening.

Split Fruit

This is something that can happen to your fruits whether you grow them inside or outside.

Split fruit occurs when the soil around the roots is allowed to get very dry, and then your plants get a sudden amount of water. For example, from a very heavy shower or a watering can.

The roots will then suck up all the water and distribute it all around the tomato plant as quickly as possible. Once the water is in the fruits, they will suddenly expand, and this causes the fruits to split.

The best way to avoid this from happening, is to water your plants regularly, and not allow the soil to dry out for long periods.

If you are growing your tomatoes outside, water thoroughly twice a week. If there is a sudden downpour, the plants won't need to absorb all that water, and the fruits won't split.

Plants are like us, they need to be kept hydrated.

WHEN AND HOW TO HARVEST YOUR TOMATOES

Tomatoes can be harvested from July all the way through to the middle of October.

All the tomatoes I've ever come across start off green, and then turn another colour when they are ripe. They can be: red, yellow, orange, purple, pink, stripped or duel coloured. Therefore it's easy to tell when your tomatoes are ripe and ready to be harvested.

However, there are some tomatoes, like Green Zebra, Sun green, Cherokee Green and any other green tomato varieties, that are ripe when they are green. So how do you know when your green tomatoes are ripe?

All you have to do is give each tomato a gentle squeeze between your finger and thumb. If the tomato feels soft, and you can squeeze it easily, then it's ripe. If the tomato still feels hard, then leave it on the plant as it's not ready.

Harvesting your ripe tomatoes is very easy. If you look just above the fruit, you will notice a small joint, this is called the "Knuckle". Holding the ripe tomato in your hand. Gently tip the fruit upwards, and the knuckle will break. You will then have your wonderful ripe tomato in your hand.

Tomatoes are best kept at room temperature as this helps them keep their rich flavour. Putting your tomatoes in a fridge takes away all that wonderful flavour and they taste very bland.

GROWING TOMATOES IN RAISED BEDS

Tomatoes will grow very successfully in raised beds. If you want to grow the cordon variety, make sure the stake is secured well in the soil, otherwise your tomato plant will fall over due to the weight of your fruits growing.

Bush varieties of tomatoes will grow very well round the edges of your raised beds. Plant your tomato plants as close to the edge of your raised bed as you can, and space your tomato plants 12 inches apart from each other. This will give your plants plenty of room to spread. As they grow, the plants will cascade over, softening the harsh edges.

Make sure you water your plants thoroughly, at least 2 or 3 times a week. During very hot weather you may have to water more often.

Also feeding your tomatoes in raised beds is very important. But check the instructions on the feed bottle, because it will tell you how often you need to feed your plants.

Bush tomatoes are also very easy to harvest when grown around the edges of a raised bed, no stretching involved. However, they are very tasty, and you'll find that every time you walk past them, you'll pick a couple to eat. How many will actually make it inside your house and to the dinner table is another matter.

TOMATO RECIPE

Tomatoes are a fruit that we use so often, but usually we buy them in cans and use as part of a sauce for pasta, or in casseroles.

When harvesting your own tomatoes, this is a complete waste of their full flavour, and the best, and to be honest, then only way to eat freshly harvested tomatoes is to have them just as they are and in a salad.

I hope this doesn't sound too boring, but with a little bit of imagination, a salad, even if it's just with tomatoes, can be so bright and colourful as well as taste amazing. Cutting your tomatoes in different ways will really bring your tomato salad to life.

Ingredients

- Get a wonderful selection of tomatoes, making sure you have as many different sizes and colours as you can get.
- Sea salt and coarsely ground pepper
- Olive oil

Method

1. Wash all your tomatoes and pat them dry with a tea towel.
2. Get a pretty plate to display your wonderful tomatoes on. A white one is best, as it contrasts with your tomatoes beautifully.
3. It's always best to start with your largest tomatoes first. So if you have some beefsteak tomatoes, take out the hard core at the top and then slice your tomatoes. Make each slice about 1cm thick. Lay the slices over the plate.
4. Next, take any medium sized tomatoes and cut them in quarters and sprinkle them over the slices.
5. If you have any tomatoes that are between cherry sized and medium sized, then just cut them in half and sprinkle on the plate as well.
6. The cherry tomatoes, just leave whole and sprinkle over the top.
7. Sprinkle a little sea salt and ground pepper over the top of the tomatoes, and then drizzle with some olive oil.
8. Cover with cling film and leave at room temperature for about 20 minutes so all the flavours can blend together. Do not cover with foil, as the acid from the tomatoes reacts with the foil and your tomatoes will have a metallic taste to them, not nice.

If you have a glut of tomatoes and can't eat them all, then you can always freeze your tomatoes so you can still enjoy them later in the year. Weigh out approximately 1lb of tomatoes and put them in a plastic bag with a twisty on top. Then when you need to make a tomato sauce, you'll have some tomatoes all ready and won't need to open a can.

WEBSITES & USEFUL LINKS

If you enjoyed this book, please leave a RATING or a REVIEW at the online store where you bought it. These make it more visible on site and will help me to keep making them!

This book is just the beginning of your growing journey. There's so much more to discover:

- I have over 300 videos for you on my YouTube page. Pop by and let me know if you have any questions: https://www.youtube.com/user/clairesallotment
- I blog regularly and I'm always delighted to hear from you (and you can sign up to my newsletter here, too): https://clairesallotment.com/
- If you have any questions about this book (or if you spot any typos!), please don't hesitate to contact my tech wizards at clairesallotment@gmail.com

- Frost dates for your garden in the UK, USA and Australia: http://www.gardenaction.co.uk/main/weather.asp

BIBLIOGRAPHY

These are the main gardening books that I refer to all the time:

The New Vegetable and Garden Expert, by Dr. D.G. Hessayon (Expert, 2014)

Pippa's Organic Kitchen Garden, by Pippa Greenwood (Dorling Kindersley, 1999) - quite old, and no longer in print, but there are second-hand copies for sale online

50 Ways to Kill a Slug, by Sarah Ford (Hamlyn, 2003)

THE LOTTIE AND DOTTIE BOOKS

"This sweet little story about the joys of growing your own vegetables is told in a clear and fuss-free text that is perfect to developing readers..."
The Guardian's Best New Children's Books Guide on Lottie & Dottie Sow Carrots

For the younger gardener in your family, these books tell delightful stories, while providing clear instructions on how to grow carrots, sunflowers and pumpkins. They also feature wonderful full colour illustrations by Marijke van Veldhoven.

Available in all good bookshops and online

Printed in Dunstable, United Kingdom

67483776R00234